Tailing Mulligan

Tailing Mulligan

Mastering the Art of Workplace Communication

Robert K. Skacel, Jr., Ph.D.

iUniverse, Inc.

New York Lincoln Shanghai

Tailing Mulligan
Mastering the Art of Workplace Communication

iUniverse, Inc.

For information address:
iUniverse, Inc.
2021 Pine Lake Road, Suite 100
Lincoln, NE 68512
www.iuniverse.com

ISBN: 0-595-30658-6

Printed in the United States of America

To my parents, Bob and Patty Skacel, who showed me what matters.

Contents

Preface

Although I hate to admit it, I have probably learned twice as much from my mistakes as I have from my achievements. This has proven true both personally and professionally, and it's been most evident when it comes to dealing with people.

Think about it. Success depends heavily on how effectively we interact with others. And the cornerstone of human interaction is communication—what we say…how we say it…what we fail to say…and what we communicate through our actions. Behavioral science tells us the strongest predictor of marital success is a couple's communication effectiveness. And except for those of us who have no co-workers, supervisors, subordinates, or customers, our success in the workplace is critically dependent on communication as well.

I have occasionally attended "Quest for Excellence," the annual conference for the Malcolm Baldrige National Quality Award, in which the winners of what is arguably the most prestigious business award in the world share their best practices. I distinctly recall a moment in one of the general sessions a few years ago, when the CEO of an award-winning company was asked to describe what he felt was the single-most important factor in achieving business excellence. Without a moment's hesitation, he answered, "Communication. You can never over-communicate!" He went on to describe how his organization deliberately and systematically fostered open and direct communication—at all levels.

Without a doubt, workplace communication is serious business, so why address such an important subject through a lighthearted fable? What does a level-headed, career-minded person stand to gain by reading a humorous tale in which the characters are not even human? Well, as any effective teacher knows, ideas sometimes stick best when they are presented in an uncommon or unexpected fashion, and when they somehow strike an emotional chord, be it one of laughter, tenderness or even pain. That's why the fables Aesop authored twenty-six hundred years ago still resonate in the postmodern mind. It's why *Animal Farm* stands among the most well-known works on totalitarianism, as does *Who Moved My Cheese?* among works on change management. Perhaps Dr. Seuss was really onto something when he said, "I like nonsense; it wakes up the brain cells."

My own education on the importance of workplace communication began with my first job at age fifteen, when I was employed as an airplane washer and errand boy with a small charter operation at an international airport.

One day I was handed a push broom and instructed to sweep the hangar floor. If you've never stood inside an airplane hangar with a broom in your hands, then you might not appreciate why I quickly found myself cursing the day I was born. That is, not unless you've tried mowing your lawn with a pair of tweezers, or painting your house with a Q-tip. Two hours and thirteen blisters into the job, I discovered I was only supposed to sweep a small portion of the floor. From this experience, I learned to ask questions.

My "schooling" continued through my first managerial job, when I worked as a clinical psychologist and supervised a team of professional clinicians at a small outpatient mental health operation. I cannot count the number of times when I wished I could have turned back the clock and taken a fresh crack at communicating an impending change, dealing with a performance issue, running a meeting, or crafting a memo. Luckily, I had a forgiving team and a boss who tolerated my errors. Nowadays I teach and coach others, from business executives to pastors, to communicate and lead more effectively; however, there is always more to learn myself.

Tailing Mulligan is a business book, yet it was written not only for executives and managers, but for all those whose work brings them in contact with other people, regardless of their level or rank. The only other things you need in order to benefit from this book are a genuine desire to improve yourself and your work environment, an attitude of respect for others, and a willingness to see the humor in life.

I wrote *Tailing Mulligan* with three objectives in mind. First, I hope you will learn valuable principles and extract practical guidance that can be used to communicate more effectively at work. Second, I hope to illustrate the value of a coaching or mentoring relationship, so you might be encouraged to seek relationships that serve to enhance your professional development. And finally, I want to accomplish the first two goals in a manner that is both entertaining and fun, so you can experience as much pleasure in the learning process as in the results. Besides, there's something to be said for learning from someone *else's* mistakes!

Rob Skacel

Acknowledgements

This book would not have been possible without the help of several dear friends, colleagues, business associates, and family members. Special thanks to Donna Queen, Todd Frick, and David Woolverton, who affirmed my work and challenged me to stay the course; to Michael Murray, Jane Dutton, Peggy Van Schaick, David Ashcraft, Dan Hobson, Ned Pelger, Jim Lowe, Mike DePietro, and Craig Lucas, who provided encouraging words, practical guidance, and editorial feedback as I attempted to develop and refine the early drafts of my manuscript. Thanks also to Elli Zeamer and Ken Murray for their assistance in editing the later drafts, and to Susan Blue, Bob Coppadge, Roger North, and Jen Litwiller, for their helpful commentary as I drew nearer to the finish line.

I owe a huge debt of gratitude to my wife Marita, and to our children Abraham, Joelle, and Elijah. My hours at the computer screen required them to sacrifice our time together, yet they were consistently understanding and supportive. And finally, I thank God, who brings purpose and pleasure to my life, grants me countless "mulligans," and forever challenges me to grow. May this book somehow reflect his goodness and grace.

1

A True Scrapper

Carson Ridge was the kind of Midwestern town nobody really loved, yet few ever left. Originally settled in the mid-1800s as "Petropolis," it later took on the name of its most famous citizen, Colonel Wesley Carson, who rode with George Custer during the American Civil War. The good colonel once stymied a confederate ambush and was credited with saving the lives of five hundred Union soldiers.

Anyone close to the events of that day knew, however, the true hero was none other than "Scrappi," a nervous and mangy refugee cat who attached herself to Carson outside Gettysburg in July of 1863. For the remainder of the war, whenever the Union soldiers camped, Scrappi would spend each morning wandering off in search of food. Her typical fare was rodents, birds, and bugs. But one crisp autumn day, as the men had just broken camp to resume the march, Scrappi was nowhere to be found. Moments later, she bounded into Carson's saddle as he rode near the head of the column. As he pet the little feline, the observant officer noticed residue of fresh grits dangling from Scrappi's whiskers. *Well*, she wouldn't have gotten *grits* from the *Yankees*! That could mean only one thing. The Confederates were nearby, and they had just fed Scrappi her breakfast! The quick-thinking Carson immediately put his men on alert and in short order, managed to put the Rebels on the run.

So after the war, the citizens of Petropolis renamed their town in honor of the Colonel, and erected a statue of his likeness on the square.

Scrappi got squat, and died a penniless stray.

But the legend of Scrappi lived on, and by the early 1920s, the story of her heroism inspired the founding of what would become the largest pet products company in the world: South Carson Ridge Animal & Pet Products, Inc., (aka "S.C.R.A.P.P.I"), headquartered three miles due south of Colonel Wesley Carson's rigidified likeness.

SCRAPPI eventually became the cornerstone of Carson Ridge's economy. When SCRAPPI did well, Carson Ridge thrived. But when SCRAPPI faltered, its citizens, people and pets alike, suffered.

Jerry Mulligan was a fourth-generation SCRAPPI employee, or "scrapper" as they came to be known. For as long as he could remember, Jerry knew he'd join the company some day. It was though he'd been bred and raised for no other purpose. So, two weeks after earning his diploma, Jerry began the daily ritual of punching in at 7 a.m. His first assignment was in the distribution center, loading the trucks that transported SCRAPPI's wares to the world. It was a dog's life, but Jerry determined he'd make the best of it.

Jerry's father had died a few years earlier, the unfortunate victim of an industrial accident. While welding a rafter high above the mixing room floor, the poor fellow toppled thirty feet into a bin of ostrich feed and suffocated. Tragedies like this were not uncommon in SCRAPPI's plants. What black lung and cave-ins were to West Virginia mining towns, lost limbs and suffocation were to Carson Ridge.

Ralph Hurley was an older worker who had been a good friend of Jerry's father. As teenagers, the two were hired by SCRAPPI on the same day. Ralph was a delivery driver who had a lot of contact with the workers on the loading docks. Because he had been close to Jerry's father, he felt a special obligation to look out for Jerry, so he took young Mulligan under his wing. Most of the dock workers looked up to Ralph—the old veteran really knew his stuff. He was still swift and strong, and could outpace most everyone when it came to lifting and moving packages. Ralph often helped the others load trucks, even though it wasn't in his job description.

Jerry and Ralph worked in the Deliscuit division, which produced tasty bakery-quality treats for "high class" pampered pets. This was not your typical doggie biscuit concocted from low-grade cereals and slaughterhouse scraps. The Deliscuit brand was the real McCoy…premium baked goods rivaling the best mother ever pulled from her oven!

Jerry was proud to work on the Deliscuit line, especially since he handled the gourmet cookies, which were the best-selling Deliscuit product. In fact, Jerry was getting so good at loading cookies onto trucks that he could toss them precisely into place from nearly ten paces out. Jerry discovered that using a high arc maximized accuracy, allowing him to outpace those who kept their cookies down. Jerry was one of the most productive of the eight hundred workers in the distribution center. He was even closing in on the cookie-tossing productivity record Ralph had set fourteen years earlier. The only problem with tossing cookies, aside from the obvious, is the further you chuck them, the greater the likelihood of breakage. So while a talented cookie-tosser might set productivity records, he or she is also more likely to damage the product.

SCRAPPI had relatively equal numbers of male and female employees, although most of the dock workers were male. Interestingly, the manager of the first shift dock workers and drivers was Michele Izhard, a recent graduate of the B.I.T. School of Management. This did not sit well with Ralph, who had a hard time respecting any female in a position of authority, much less as his own boss.

Michele was happy to see Jerry and the others tossing cookies so quickly and efficiently, but she expressed concern about the high breakage rates. Customers appreciated prompt deliveries, but didn't like to open boxes filled with broken cookies. So, predictably, Michele started monitoring breakage rates along with productivity.

Jerry and his co-workers frequently complained to each other about how disorganized and asinine the loading process was, and how management ought to devise a method to improve it. In fact, Jerry even figured the cookie-tossing dock workers could decrease breakage rates and perhaps even increase loading productivity with two simple changes:

1. Pack the cookies in bubble-wrap rather than wax paper.

2. Add casters to the bottom pallet of each stack of boxed cookies. This would decrease the cookie-toss distance by enabling workers to wheel the boxes right into the trucks for loading. Nonetheless, the cookie-tossers seemed to enjoy griping and growling amongst themselves, and though they never brought their ideas to management, they hoped Michele would someday discover ways of improving the loading process. After all, wasn't that what she was hired for?

Ralph, in particular, resented Michele's exhortations about breakage and productivity. To him, management was a nuisance...and this *Michele*, who couldn't have been more than twenty five years old, and had probably never loaded a truck in her life...who was *she* to be looking over his shoulder, telling *him* how to do his job? Ralph detested her, and everyone knew it.

Jerry sometimes found himself sympathizing with Michele. She seemed to be trying her best, but Ralph never cut her a break. He constantly ridiculed Michele in her absence and sometimes openly challenged her authority. Jerry was impressed with Michele's apparent ability to let Ralph's comments roll off her back. He wondered, though, if beneath Michele's hardened exterior, she might actually be hurting.

Jerry always walked a straight line whenever Michele was around. To see them interact, one might even think they enjoyed each other's company. They would smile and joke together, and usually seemed to agree on how to deal with the day-to-day problems that would arise on the docks. Jerry truly appreciated the difficulty of Michele's job, and found himself developing a certain level of respect for her abilities. But when Michele was away from the loading area, Jerry joined the others in making fun of her. He railed, sometimes mercilessly, on her looks, her mannerisms, her reptilian personality...you name it. The guys laughed at Jerry's cracks, and since Michele wasn't there to hear them, Jerry figured there was really no harm done.

Things went on this way until one day Michele announced changes would be made. She produced a few graphs and charts showing that while the Deliscuit cookie-tossers had indeed accomplished the highest truck-loading productivity rates in the company, their product breakage rates were eight times higher, on average, than the other divisions, and one hundred thirty seven times higher than the highest performer, the chew toy division. She also announced Ralph's deliveries consistently had the highest breakage rates, more than three times that of the other Deliscuit drivers. Ralph was demoted from driver to packer, and the cookie-tossing dock workers were asked to improve their breakage rates, even if it meant a slight decline in loading productivity.

"Whaaat!?" thought Jerry. "How can she get away with this?" To him, this seemed absolutely ridiculous! Sure, the cookie-tossers could improve their breakage rates by slowing down a bit, but Deliscuit cookies are simply more delicate than the other products.

Of *course* the breakage rates were higher than the chew toy rates—you couldn't break a chew toy if you shot it from a cannon into a concrete wall!

And why was Michele persecuting Ralph? Ralph *had* been a little tough on her, but he hadn't done anything that warranted a two-level demotion! And, if a guy had high breakage rates as a *driver*, why on *earth* would you make him a *packer*!?

Ralph apologized to the cookie-tossers for getting them in trouble. He told them how Michele called him into her office the day before—how she "snapped" at him for constantly making her look bad in front of the others. In Ralph's estimation, this cold-blooded, insecure, and incompetent manager was making him an example, and was punishing the others for no other reason than to ensure they would "understand who's boss."

Any sympathy Jerry felt for Michele was now gone. She became the enemy. Ralph was right all along—management *was* a bunch of idiots!

Jerry's attitude deteriorated steadily and the entire shift's morale began to decline. Jerry decided he would simply do what he was told, nothing more, nothing less. He no longer took pride in his work. Who cared if he could load boxes faster than anyone else? Why bother to decrease breakage rates? He'd never get ahead anyway. The managers would just find more ways to make everyone else's life more difficult, and would pick on anyone they felt threatened by. Ralph Hurley was proof of that.

The animosity in the distribution center became unbearable. Though one might expect that among *wild* animals, it was wholly uncharacteristic of the domesticated sorts that populated SCRAPPI's workforce. In case you hadn't guessed, Jerry Mulligan was not just another blue-collar dock worker. He was literally a blue-collared dog worker...specifically, an Irish setter. Thin, spirited, intelligent, and full of energy (not to mention white teeth, shiny coat, and strong bones), Jerry was a mere house pet. The

SCRAPPI corporation was founded on the simple principle that no one could meet the needs of household pets better than pets themselves. So, from the CEO (a piranha named Rae Zorr) to the mail clerk, every employee was a pet.

Michele Izhard was a turtle. In fact, her office was a little plastic island aquarium with artificial palm trees and a lagoon. On rough days, Michele would put her phone on "Do Not Disturb," and dive underwater for extended periods of constructive escape. Jerry was right, her tough outer shell belied a tender and sensitive inner-self.

Ralph Hurley was a falcon raised in captivity. He was featured in an Orlando-area bird show as a youngster, but at the first chance of escape, Ralph stowed away on a SCRAPPI truck that had just unloaded musical instruments for a certain killer whale and his "orca-stra." At the end of the line, when the trailer door opened at the dock to reveal a company run completely by animals, young Ralph knew he had found his new home. That was a long time ago. SCRAPPI changed since then, and so did Ralph.

Jerry continued to resent Michele more with each passing day. To his way of thinking, she should have sensed he was frustrated with his work. She should have known he felt unfairly treated, that her demands were too great, that he was angry for the way she'd handled Ralph. How could she be so clueless? Jerry wondered if perhaps Michele suffered neurological damage from spending too much time with her head retracted into her shell.

Things remained that way for several weeks. That is, until "bring your children to work day." Michele had two little ones—Ella and Sam. They were generally well-behaved, but like any youngsters in strange surroundings, they got a little too curious. Ella and Sam remained by their mother's side for most of the morning. When Michele became busy with a lengthy phone call, the two young turtles slipped out of her office unnoticed, and made a bee-line (albeit slower than your average bee); to a large crate of Deliscuit snickerdoodle cookies that Ralph Hurley just finished packing. One of the worst things you could have at a food distribution center was a Sam and Ella outbreak, so when Ralph caught Sam and Ella rummaging through the cookies, he went ballistic! Jerry tried to calm him, but to no avail. Ralph grabbed the tearful little Ella in his talons and scolded her in the harshest of tones. Michele heard the commotion and burst out of her office. She and Ralph really got into it. Ralph's job was now on the line.

That was the last straw for Jerry. Sure, Ralph lost his temper, but nobody got hurt. And those two little reptiles had truly made a mess of Ralph's work. After a few moments of agitated pacing, Jerry marched right into Michele's office to give her a piece of his mind. He held nothing back. He spewed forth such a litany of criticisms, accusations, and complaints, he began to foam at the mouth. Each time Michele tried to respond, he interrupted and continued his tirade. When he was through, Jerry stormed out of Michele's office, slammed the door behind him, and walked off the premises. He didn't know where he was going, but he knew he had to walk.

Two miles later, Jerry began to settle down as he took stock of what happened. Jerry felt justified. After all, he was merely sticking up for a good friend, right? Ralph had been unfairly treated, hadn't he? In any event, Jerry realized he had to find another job.

As he passed a corner shop known as Monty's Snack Shack, Jerry decided to stop in to see the proprietor's niece, a boa constrictor named Alice. Alice was always such a good listener—patient, reflective, and never judgmental—and boy could she give a good hug! Just what Jerry needed at that moment. As they spoke, Uncle Monty (a python related to Alice through marriage) brought out bottled water and cookies for Jerry and Alice to share. Wouldn't you know it, Deliscuit brand. These particular treats were like animal crackers. Naturally, Alice favored the goldfish and mice, while Jerry preferred the cats.

As they continued to talk and eat, Jerry noticed most of the Deliscuit biscuits were broken. Sure, boxes of cookies always contain a few damaged ones, but Jerry could hardly find any intact. He wondered why. He motioned to Uncle Monty.

"Heh, heh, heh," chuckled Monty. "These are the last of the ones I used to get from Ralph Hurley when he delivered in this area. Old Ralph used to give me a good deal on damaged goods. Strictly a cash arrangement, but definitely worth it."

Jerry wondered about this. He knew broken products could be given to charities, or to employees' friends and family, but company policy strictly prohibited selling them, even at discounted rates. After all, as the industry leader in premium baked goods for pets, SCRAPPI had a reputation to uphold.

"Yeah," Monty continued, "Ralph had a pretty good thing going. Not just with me, but with several others as well. Along with my regular orders, I'd always buy quantities of broken Deliscuits at half price. I'd mix them in with the good ones. It was a win-win situation. I wound up with better profit margins, and Ralph walked away with a little extra pocket change. It worked out pretty well until his boss found out about it...some turtle named 'Shelly' I think."

Jerry corrected him. "It's Michele."

"Whatever. Anyway, that was the end of Ralph's driving days. I tried to make a similar deal with the new guy, but he wouldn't think of it."

Jerry suddenly felt a huge lump in his throat, and it wasn't because of the half-chewed Deliscuit working its way down his esophagus. At that very moment he realized the situation with Ralph figured wrong. The high breakage rates, Ralph's trouble with Michele, the demotion...Michele *hadn't* persecuted Ralph. Ralph brought it on himself! Michele simply caught him in dishonest dealings.

Jerry felt angry, betrayed. Ralph Hurley lied to him all along, and he bought it: hook, line, and sinker. And after Jerry's antics earlier that day, it would now likely cost Jerry *his* career with SCRAPPI, too. Why hadn't Michele told him about this? She could have saved herself a lot of grief. She knew Ralph was lying to the others, but she just let it continue. Jerry felt sorry for himself, and terrible for the way he treated Michele.

Like many of us in such situations, Jerry wished he could go back in time and do it all over again…only the *right* way *this* time. Jerry sat there for a few moments, completely dumbfounded. Then he regained composure, said good-bye to Alice, and walked to his apartment. He crashed face-down on his bed, drooling ever so slightly from the left side of his lower lip, his thoughts racing a mile a minute.

All he could do was pray: "Dear God, what have I done? I wanted nothing more than to do good work, be a decent guy, and take care of my friends. Somehow I goofed everything up. I wish there was something I could do to make it right. I know I got myself into this mess, but if there's any way to fix things, please show it to me. If not, then please help me to learn from it, and salvage some kind of future for my career."

2

Second Chance

Jerry laid on the bed a few moments in silence. Suddenly and without warning, he felt an uncontrollable urge to bark, so he knew someone must be outside his apartment door. And then came a knock.

"Come in."

The door swung open to reveal an elderly border collie, probably in her mid-seventies. But that was about five hundred in dog years, so this pooch was the canine equivalent of Methuselah! She wore nothing but a kind smile and a threadbare bandanna around her neck. The graying around her eyes and mouth gave her a look of wisdom, and she walked with a slight limp, protecting her right front paw.

"Jerry Mulligan?" she asked. Jerry nodded. "Your prayers have been heard. I am Sophia, sent to be your fairy godmother."

"Sounds good to me, but I thought only humans could be godmothers."

"Well, technically, I'm your fairy *dog*mother. But Henderson in HR assigns the job titles, and he's got a touch of dyslexia. So, godmother it is. Get used to it."

"Okay…" said Jerry, trying to go with the flow, yet not quite sure what to make of the situation.

"Anyway, Jerry, you seem to have gotten yourself into a bit of a jam."

"You know about my situation?"

"Of course I do."

"But how?"

"It would take me a while to explain. Let's just say in my line of work, you never get an assignment without first receiving a thorough briefing."

"Okey-dokey," said Jerry. He was beginning to get a little nervous now, wondering if maybe Monty had slipped something into his water at the Snack Shack.

"Relax, Mulligan," said Sophia. "Like I said, I'm here to help."

Jerry decided to play along. What did he have to lose? He began, "Well Sophia, I *am* in a jam...a *terrible* one. But I don't know how I could have seen it coming. It all seemed so clear, but this afternoon when I was with my friend Alice and her uncle, everything I thought I knew turned out to be false. I'm still trying to sift through it in my mind."

"Jerry, I can help you on this. But it will mean you'll have to make some changes in the ways you think about and behave toward others. Are you willing to do this?"

"Just exactly what are you asking of me?"

"I know this might be hard for you to believe, but I've been given the power to grant you a 'mulligan'...a do-over...a chance to turn back the clock and start fresh. You'll not only be able to *learn* from your mistakes, but to literally re-live and revise them...as if they'd never occurred in the first place."

"Get out of town!" said Jerry, in disbelief.

"Sometimes I'd like to," Sophia responded. "But good jobs are pretty hard for dogs to find outside of Carson Ridge, and I just don't have the energy or bladder control these days to go around marking off new territory. Look, Jerry, you're in a fix *now* because of things you did and assumptions you made a long time ago. I can take you back to the beginning of this mess and coach you through it as you go along."

"Well, all right."

"Jerry, do you see this?" Sophia bore the pads of her right paw in which she was clutching a gnarly, half-chewed slab of dehydrated cow skin. "This is a *magic* rawhide chew. By waving it in the air, I can turn back the clock or freeze any moment in time. When we need to talk, I can either stop things altogether, or I can coach you as the situation continues. When we're in the middle of a work-place situation, I'll speak in italics, *like this*, so no one else will be able to hear me. No one besides you will see me either."

"Wow, I thought jet lag was a hassle. This is going to get confusing. How will I know whether we're moving forward, backward, or standing still?"

"You know how to operate a DVD player, don't you? Here. From now on you will wear these glasses. Put them on."

Jerry complied.

"Can you see the LCD display in the lower left corner of your field of vision?" Sophia asked.

"Yep."

"Here's how it works. This symbol means 'PAUSE.' When you see it, you'll know time has been frozen.

"This one is 'REWIND.' It will take us back in time.

"This one is 'FAST FORWARD,' which we will use to return quickly to the present.

"And finally, 'PLAY.' Whenever the 'PLAY' indicator is on, so is your life. Got it?"

"I think so…kind of like *It's a Wonderful Life*, *Back to the Future*, and *Groundhog Day* all rolled into one."

"Sort of. Are you with me?"

"Why not?"

"Good. Then let's get started. In a little while, I'm going to take you back to the day when Michele announced her concerns about the high breakage rates. And this time, we're going to get it right. We've got a lot of cleaning up to do, but before we go, I want to talk with you about a few things."

"Sure."

"Jerry, do you remember when you, Igor, and Milt stood around complaining about the loading process?"

"Yeah, we did that all the time."

"Why?"

"I don't know, Sophia." Jerry paused to think. "It really was a stupid set-up. They could have made it so much better."

"So, what was your purpose? What were the three of you trying to accomplish through your whining?"

"What were we trying to *accomplish*? We weren't trying to *accomplish* anything! We were just blowing off steam…venting to each other. What's wrong with that?"

"Jerry, you have nieces and nephews, don't you?"

"Yeah, they're cute little pups."

"Do they ever whine and complain?"

"Not very often, but when they do, it drives me nuts. Like the other night. I was visiting my sister's family for dinner. In the middle of the meal, little Kelly starts whining about her fork being bent. You had to hold it half an inch from your snout to even see it wasn't straight. And there must have been a million other forks in the drawer by the counter, but she just went on and on about that one stupid fork. I got so irritated I snapped at my sister, 'WOULD SOMEBODY PLEASE GET THIS LITTLE MONGREL ANOTHER FORK!?' I mean, come on! In those two minutes, Kelly could have run back and forth to that drawer twenty times herself and gotten enough forks for the next three months!"

"So when your niece was just 'venting' like that, and you complained to your sister, I suppose your sister just got up and retrieved a new fork."

"No, my sister said Kelly had to learn to solve problems herself. And if she would have stepped in and gotten a new fork for Kelly, she would have only reinforced Kelly's whining rather than teach her about solving problems. She eventually asked Kelly a few questions about what could be done to improve the situation and Kelly figured she could just get her own new fork."

"Your sister must be a wise parent. It sounds like she was careful not to reinforce *your* complaining either."

"So you're saying by criticizing the loading process without offering any solutions, I was acting like a five-year-old with a bent fork?"

"That's what I'm saying, Jerry."

> # It is futile to complain and criticize unless you are willing to do something to improve the situation.

"Well," Jerry paused as he was simultaneously defending his behavior, yet trying to digest Sophia's counsel. "As I said a little while ago, they could have made the process better. I even had some ideas that would have sped things up *and* reduced the breakage rates."

"Who are *they*?"

"You know…the management."

"And what did *they* say when you presented your ideas to them?"

"Well, I never really said anything to them. Look, it's up to management to make those calls. That's why they get paid the big bucks. I just want to toss my cookies and be left alone."

"Is that really what you want, Jerry? Look, you've got some ideas that might lead to improvement. Maybe Michele and the other managers would have considered them, or maybe not. But one thing I know for sure—your good ideas don't stand much chance of being implemented unless you either try them yourself or tell them to someone else who might have the power to put them in place."

> # If you have something to say, tell it to someone who can take action.

"Jerry, you can't expect others to read your mind, no matter where they fit in the organizational chart. Everybody's job is difficult enough without your adding *clairvoyance* to their job descriptions."

"I never thought about it that way. I guess I didn't give Michele a fair shot. But you know what still puzzles me?"

"What's that?"

"If Michele *knew* Ralph was selling the broken cookies and keeping the money himself…and if that was the real reason she demoted him, why didn't she just tell us? If she had, I would have never taken Ralph's side, and I sure would not have given her the Cujo treatment this morning either."

"Remember, Jerry, there are two sides to every story."

"My mother always used to tell me that. I once threw that phrase back on her when we had a disagreement, but somehow my father and his rolled-up newspaper took her side, and I felt the consequences on my hind side."

"Seriously, Jerry…any manager who has ever been involved in a delicate employee discipline situation knows they must be very careful to handle things as cleanly as possible…that they can't disclose details of the situation to other employees. Even a simple, benign error in judgment on the company's part can leave the door open for the unscrupulous to do a lot of damage through 'legal' channels. Besides, why should Michele stoop to Ralph's level? Maybe she values others enough to leave them their dignity when they've goofed up. Maybe she realizes how humiliating it can be to scold someone publicly. Maybe she's got more character than you've given her credit for. You see, there could be lots of reasons why Michele wouldn't tell you what she knew about Ralph's dishonest behavior. And Ralph knew that, so he played you and the others like a banjo at a Tennessee hoe-down."

> # There are some things management simply *cannot* and should not disclose.

"Let's go back so I can do it right this time," Jerry said, eager to fix things.

"You know, Jerry, there's one more critical lesson you must learn before you can return to the past."

"I hope it's a simple one, because right now my brain is on overload. I haven't had this much to remember since obedience school."

"This one may be a little tough for you to swallow, but stay with me for a minute. You're a dog, right?"

"Right. I'm with you so far."

"And dogs are known for their loyalty, right?"

"Yeah…?"

"Why did you speak so poorly of Michele when she wasn't around? I mean, you acted like you respected her when you were with her, but the moment she turned her back, you said some horribly derogatory things about her."

"I knew you were going to nail me for that. What I did was wrong. But for some reason, it's just really hard to confront others face-to-face. They may take things personally, feel hurt, or even get angry. At least when you gossip, you don't have that whole defensiveness thing to deal with."

"That's pretty weak, Jerry," responded Sophia. "Besides, you not only damaged the trust between yourself and Michele, you also proved yourself untrustworthy to Igor and Milt. You see, they'll assume if you are willing to talk behind Michele's back—though you treat her as a friend in her presence—you must also be willing to speak poorly of them when they're not around…and they're probably right about that."

> **If you talk behind the backs of some, others will wonder what you say about them when *they* are not around…and you will lose their trust.**

"Gee, Sophia, you really don't mince words."

"Jerry, I promise to be direct with you, even when it's difficult. If you can live with that, you may really go places some day."

"I'll try, but maybe you could be a little easier on me. After all, I'm new at this."

"It's a deal. Now I think you're ready to go back and do this whole thing over again."

Sophia took Jerry back to the beginning. He tried his best to handle the situation differently this time. And though Jerry didn't do a perfect job with Sophia's coaching, the end result was much better. Instead of complaining, Jerry offered to help solve the problems he identified. The company even implemented Jerry's idea of placing casters on the bottom-most pallets, though his bubble-wrap suggestion was rejected after some consideration, given it would take too much extra packing space.

Michele conceded it was unreasonable to expect the same low breakage rates for Deliscuits as for chew-toys, but the communication improvements between the managers and cookie-tossers paved the way for a more collaborative approach to maximizing productivity while keeping breakage to a minimum.

Perhaps most importantly, Jerry was recognized for his positive attitude, problem-solving abilities, and trustworthiness. Instead of being out of a job, he was beginning to develop genuine leadership credibility on behalf of his peers, and in the eyes of the managers.

Of course, Sophia appeared at various points to help Jerry through the toughest moments, but Jerry also began to experience the value of effective communication. There would be more lessons. He knew that all too well.

As they began to wrap up the Ralph Hurley situation once and for all, Jerry said, "Sophia, I don't quite know how to thank you. Will I see you again? I have a feeling I'll need a few more mulligans."

"I'll be here if you need me."

"How can I get a hold of you?"

"Here, take this magic dog whistle. Whenever you blow it, I'll know you need my help, and I'll get here as quickly as I can."

"Golly, I'd better keep this in a safe place," Jerry said as he placed it in his pocket.

"Well, if you lose it, you can always email me at: sophia_pleasehelpmeigoofedupagain@trueedgeonline.com

When Sophia left, Jerry decided to jot down some reminders to help him communicate more effectively in the future. He planned to do this after each situation in which he learned something significant about workplace communication. Jerry felt if he could mull through these questions from time to time (especially when feeling upset about something at work), it might keep him from repeating past mistakes. Since he figured he might someday pass them onto others, he thought about calling them "Jerry's Pointers." But since he was an Irish setter and not a pointer, he decided on "Mulligan's Mull-Agains" instead. Here's what he came up with:

Mulligan's Mull-Agains

1. Are my facts really facts, or am I responding to unverified assumptions? Could there be another side to the story?

2. Am I helping to solve problems, or just complaining? What do I hope to accomplish by opening my mouth?

3. Am I expecting others to read my mind, or am I taking responsibility for expressing myself in a direct and constructive way?

4. Am I being as kind when I talk about others as I am when talking to them?

5. Why do I feel compelled to bark whenever someone shows up at the door?

3

A Much Anticipated Event

It was that time of year again. The dog days of summer—warm weather, long evenings, vacations, and of course, the annual SCRAPPI employee picnic. This was a major event for the entire town. With Carson Ridge as the location of SCRAPPI's corporate headquarters and some key production and distribution operations, there were more than seven thousand employees in the immediate area. And since many of the employees had multiple litters of critters, some families were rather large. This made for one huge picnic, and organizing it was a colossal task.

It had long been company policy to include employees from all levels on the picnic planning committee. This made for an event everyone could enjoy. Jerry Mulligan was asked to represent his division this year. Though involvement on the committee was a big job that required a lot of after-hours work, it was considered an honor to be invited to participate. Committees like this one were seen as proving grounds. Those asked to participate were usually under consideration for promotion. Some key managers would closely watch Jerry's performance. So naturally, he wanted to do a good job.

The picnic committee was chaired by an oscar whose name, ironically, was Oscar. Oscars aren't very good pets. They are aggressive fish and have a tendency to eat anything in their aquariums smaller than themselves. In fact, if two oscars share an aquarium, the stronger will eventually attack and kill the weaker. So, if anyone ever offers to sell you two oscars for the price of one, don't get fooled into thinking you're getting a good deal. The free one is going to die anyway, and you'll just end up wasting an extra 1.6 gallons of water disposing the carcass.

Oscar couldn't bear long meetings. He had no time for small talk, and no tolerance for tangents. He liked to get in, dole out assignments, and then move on to the next task.

Oscar intimidated Jerry. Jerry feared offering a suggestion or opinion that Oscar might not like, because the contentious fish might find a way to retaliate. As it was, Oscar did not seem to hold Jerry in high regard. He made wisecracks about Jerry's fur style, his spiked blue collar, his clothing, and the tattoo of a fire hydrant on Jerry's left hind leg. Oscar's digs were not overtly hostile, but were delivered with a certain edge that was undeniably condescending. Jerry figured the safest thing to do was open his mouth as little as possible, and speak only when spoken to. This was not a bad strategy given the circumstances, but it meant Jerry would miss the opportunity to showcase his talents. He wondered why he ever agreed to participate.

The committee had several practical matters to tackle during the first several meetings. For example, this year the company would experiment with trucking in portable toilets to accommodate the large crowd. And while there was general agreement that the pavilion nearest the johns be assigned to a species with a relatively dull sense of smell, none were willing to volunteer their own species to be closest to the feces. In the end, it fell predictably to the guinea pigs. They almost always got stuck "volunteering" for experiments like these.

Then there was the potato sack race controversy. The frogs, seemingly strong contenders in this event, had not entered a team in more than twenty years. They claimed the burlap sacks stuck to their slimy legs like a cheap set of nylons on a hot summer day, causing severe chafing and skin lesions. There were some tense exchanges between the frogs and the rabbits (who, incidentally, had fielded the winning team for the last nine consecutive years), until someone suggested sewing a non-stick lining to the inside of the burlap sacks.

Finally, there was some disagreement about what to do with the ants. This was the first year SCRAPPI had ever employed such insects. Most worked on a new product line that included ant farms, exercise equipment, and workout accessories. Some committee members feared the ants would overrun the picnic. After a brief debate, Oscar interceded.

"There are clearly two sides to this issue," he began. "And it doesn't look like we're all going to come to agreement even if we discuss this for the next three weeks. So, we'll just have to make the best decision we can based on the information available. As I see it, we have three options. We can invite all the ants, some of the ants, or none of the ants. I'd like to see us choose the most appropriate course of action…one that respects our commitment to diversity, yet minimizes any infringements upon the personal freedoms of any of the parties involved. So, that's what we'll do. Mr. Mulligan, you're in charge of sending out the invitations. Make sure the invitation list is consistent with what we have just decided here today."

Jerry was daydreaming until he heard his name, and didn't know how to respond. He wasn't entirely clear what Oscar decided. Yet, Jerry also did not want to risk looking foolish in front of Oscar and the rest of the committee. Besides, he could probably figure it out later, or ask someone to help him with the invitations. So, despite his confusion, Jerry simply said, "Will do, Mr. O."

"Well I'm glad that's settled," said Oscar. "I think we can adjourn now. See all of you at the next meeting."

Oscar swam off immediately, but others lingered so they could coordinate tasks or simply chat. Jerry approached Clipper, a former pet alligator who had been abandoned in a storm drain after he grew too large for his human master's comfort.

"Hey, Clip. I was wondering if you might be able to help me with the invitations. Now that I'm going to have to send out extras for the ants, it's turning into a bigger job than I thought." (Jerry figured the odds were two-to-one that he'd have to send some invitations to ants, given that two of the options Oscar described involved inviting at least *some* of the ants.)

"Well, let me think about it for a few minutes before I give you an *ants*wer," Clip quipped. "Seriously, is that how you understood it, Jerry? To be honest, I couldn't tell if Oscar decided to invite the ants or not. I was kind of thinking he didn't want them invited, but if you read that differently, we can do the invitations. Sure, I'll help you."

"Uh-oh," Jerry thought. "I'd better ask someone else." So he thanked Clip for his offer to help, indicated he'd be in touch soon, and made his way across the room to talk with the others. This didn't help matters, as each one Jerry spoke with seemed to have a different take on Oscar's decision. By that point, Jerry was afraid to go back to Oscar and ask for clarity. Oscar didn't seem to like him in the first place, and after acknowledging he knew what to do, Jerry would look terribly foolish approaching Oscar now.

"Well," he thought, "my first instinct was that Oscar wanted me to invite the ants…and with all the recent talk about SCRAPPI's diversity efforts, that must be what Oscar intended."

So, Jerry pulled together a few more co-workers to help, and in a masterful show of operational efficiency, processed the invitations faster than anyone could have predicted. But when the day of the picnic finally arrived, and the ants began to appear with their families, a frantic-looking Oscar darted to Jerry, his jaw tense and gills pulsating.

"Mulligan! What are all these ants doing here?! Didn't I tell you NOT to invite them? We didn't plan for all these extra mouths to feed!"

Yikes! Jerry blew it this time. As Oscar prophesied, the food ran out quickly. The hungry ants, occupying the last table called to the buffet line, made their way instead to the other pavilions and swarmed everyone else's food. Not only did the ants feel slighted, but the other workers became irritated and angry toward the ants, whom they blamed for ruining the company party.

What could Jerry do but contact Sophia? So he blew the magic whistle.

Sophia rushed to the scene as Jerry filled her in.

After listening intently, she responded, "I think I can help. You know, from what you described, it sounds like Oscar was pretty unclear, which is unusual for him. I wonder why he did that."

"I don't know," Jerry responded.

"Hmm." Sophia paused. "Jerry, you mentioned you didn't ask Oscar for clarity because you were afraid you would have looked foolish. It seems to me you wound up looking foolish anyway, but at a point when the stakes were higher. You know, sometimes you must ask questions even if you think you might look bad. If you risk botching up your job by not asking, then by all means, ask."

> **When you are unsure, seek clarification. It is better to risk asking questions at the beginning of a project than offering excuses at the end.**

"Sophia, Oscar is pretty tough to deal with. If he doesn't like where I'm heading with my questions, it could get rough."

"That's true, I guess. So you'll need to be especially careful with your presentation."

"My presentation?"

"Yes. By that, I'm referring to the way you *package* your message. I once had a fishing buddy who taught me, 'You can have the right bait or lure, but if you don't get it in front of the fish in the right way, you won't catch a thing. It's all in the presentation.' Jerry, you need to package your words carefully so as to minimize an overreaction on Oscar's part."

"That makes sense. I'll try it. But does it only work on fish?"

"No, it applies to just about all animals. Works pretty well with humans, too."

Sophia rewound to the meeting when Oscar made his decision concerning the ants.

Like last time, Oscar finished with, "…Mr. Mulligan, you're in charge of sending out the invitations. Make sure the invitation list is consistent with what we have just decided here today."

"Okay, Jerry, here's your chance," Sophia injected.

This time, Jerry pushed for a clearer message. "Mr. Oscar, I'm still a little unclear on exactly which of the three options you want us to pursue."

"Weren't you listening, Mulligan?"

"Hang tough, Jerry. Don't put him on the defensive, but be sure you get him to articulate his decision."

"I'm sorry, Mr. Oscar, I must have missed something. This is obviously a delicate situation, and I want to make sure I get it straight. Which of the three options did you decide on?"

"Nice! By apologizing first and then affirming the importance of accurately hearing what Oscar has to say, you're building him up rather than attacking. You're helping him to notch down his defensiveness and negative emotions."

Oscar hesitated and looked a bit frustrated. After more hemming and hawing, he eventually said, "I'm telling you not to invite the ants."

"Okay," said Jerry, "so you don't want me to invite ANY of the ants? Is that what you want me to do?"

"Good work, Jerry. You're leaving absolutely no room for misinterpretation for anyone in this room."

"That's right," Oscar replied.

"Mr. Oscar, if I may," Jerry asked, "Can you help me understand the basis of your decision? I'm concerned there might be a backlash, and I want to be sure I can accurately answer any questions that might arise."

"Look, Mulligan. This picnic is expensive. We've got to draw the line somewhere!"

"But I wonder if we might be inadvertently sending a bad message. Are we telling the ants they are not valued? Are we giving others subtle permission to treat the ants as 'less-than-equal?' I can't imagine we would want to do that. Isn't there some way we can pull off an enjoyable and affordable picnic and still include the ants?"

"Jerry," said Sophia, "You did a good job walking that fine line of expressing your values without coming off as morally rigid or stubborn. Depending on how strongly you feel, the potential consequences, and whether you want to choose this particular situation as your battlefield, you could push things a little further. But that's up to you to decide."

"I think I've made my point, Sophia. If Oscar is going to take a prejudicial stance on this, at least I'm going to force him to own it. I don't believe the other senior leaders will stand behind Oscar's reasoning. If they do, then I'll think about doing something a little more drastic."

"I think that's wise."

"There's something else about this whole thing that bothers me."

"What's that, Mulligan?"

"From the day I joined this committee, Oscar and others have busted on me for the way I dress, the way I groom, and for my tattoo. It's like they just don't take me seriously or respect me because I don't dress the way they do."

"Jerry, what do you want to be in this company? Are you content with what you do, or do you want to move on to something else here?"

"Well, I like my job, but I think someday I'd like to move into management. I think I have what it takes…if they only give me the chance."

"I think you have what it takes, too. And I agree…you shouldn't have your options limited by others just because of the way you dress or groom yourself. There are a lot of executives who choose to wear their hair long, dress in an unconventional fashion, or sport tattoos. Nonetheless, I'd encourage you to consider what you are communicating through your chosen appearance. You certainly have the right to express your individuality. But if you do so, you must also accept the reality that others will form opinions about you based on the way you adorn yourself. If you choose to maintain an unconventional appearance, you will have a tougher time gaining acceptance and establishing credibility in a managerial role. It's not that it can't be done, but it will be more challenging. On the other hand, if you alter your appearance to more closely fit the role you desire, you'll have an easier time getting others to accept you, but you might have more difficulty accepting yourself. It's a tough thing to balance. But rather than getting angry at the world for judging you by your appearance, make a choice, take responsibility for it, and live with the consequences. Choose your pain, and stop blaming others for the outcome."

"But I don't want to give up who I *am* just so I can get ahead."

"You should never do that. But this isn't about your ethnicity, body shape, or disability status. It's about something entirely within your own choosing. It's about a message you can elect to transmit. Why are you clinging to a certain style of dress anyway? Isn't it just as shallow and superficial for you to insist on wearing your clothes or hair a certain way, or openly displaying your tattoo, as it is for others to judge you by those things? If your chosen appearance doesn't work, then choose something that does, unless you have a good reason for bucking convention. If changing your appearance means giving up who you are, then you're pretty shallow. Like it or not, there is such a thing as a professional appearance. If you want to communicate professionalism, adopt that kind of appearance. If you don't care whether others see you as professional, then dress for whatever role you wish."

> # The appearance you choose communicates how you want others to see you; therefore, choose an appearance that matches your goals.

Jerry carefully considered Sophia's words. He decided it might be best to upgrade his wardrobe, cut his hair, and cover his tattoo. He also thought he could be more careful with his language, eliminating words like "ain't" and curbing profanity. Doing so might help him to communicate a more professional identity. As he made these changes, he actually began to see himself as more professional.

As for the picnic, Oscar thought things through more carefully, and eventually backed away from excluding the ants. Jerry certainly didn't gain any brownie points with Oscar, but he was satisfied knowing he stood up for what he knew to be right. And though Oscar didn't necessarily like Jerry, from then on, he afforded Jerry more respect.

By the way, this time the picnic came off just fine. Knowing the ants were coming, the committee prepared plenty of food. There was still inter-species tension, but SCRAPPI was one step closer to becoming the kind of company it hoped to be.

Jerry also decided to take business classes at a local university in hopes of creating more options for his future. School was tough at first—but once Jerry learned to distinguish homework papers from food, he rose to the top of his class.

Mulligan's Mull-Agains

1. Am I clear on what I've been asked to do?

2. Is my pride keeping me from getting the help or information I need to get the job done right?

3. How can I "package" my message to improve its clarity and palatability?

4. What do I hope to communicate through my chosen appearance?

5. Do fish really feel pain?

4

Lend Me Your Ears

Over the next few years, Jerry worked tirelessly—at SCRAPPI by day and the university by night. With diligent study and the help of SCRAPPI's tuition reimbursement program, Jerry managed to earn his degree quickly, and he moved through several different positions with the company, each time assuming more responsibility. He liked new challenges, and truly enjoyed his work.

During that same time, Jerry experienced substantial changes in his personal life. For two years, he'd had a stormy, romantic relationship with a primate from Clerical (those twenty fingers sure were handy when it came to typing), but it soon became apparent she wasn't the gorilla of his dreams, so he broke things off. Within a few months, he straightened out his emotions and began dating Gertrude, a quick-witted German shepherd who would eventually become his wife, best friend, and mother of his pups.

SCRAPPI's leadership always looked for ways to expand and diversify the business, and recently initiated a venture into pet sportswear. This racy line of colorful, high fashion clothing and shoes was originally called "Animal Instincts," but the folks in Marketing felt the name had sexual and violent connotations inconsistent with SCRAPPI's family-friendly image.

Next, they considered "Pet Instincts." But when this name was test marketed with consumers, it was seen as domestic and tame…better suited for a scratching post or a lint brush than for high fashion clothing.

After many attempts to find a workable compromise between those who liked the domestic image and those who favored something a little more risqué, the team settled on "P.I. Gear." The initials derived from "Pet Instincts," thus appeasing the family-friendly advocates. Yet the term "Gear" brought an added sense of flash and flare, with connotations of hard-driving-full-contact-sports-sweat-inducing-activity. Everyone was happy.

Jerry was chosen to participate on the team that would get PI Gear into production. His particular role was to coordinate the various design elements like color, fabric, and pattern selections with the manufacturing process. He reported to a one-armed newt named Isaac, who insisted his subordinates address him as "Sir." Sir Isaac the newt, was pleasant enough, but always approached his work with a certain gravity that made others uncomfortable. Isaac grew up in the same aquarium as Oscar, which explains why he was missing an arm.

Years ago, when young Oscar's owner once forgot to feed him, that hungry predator launched a surprise attack against Isaac. The newt was caught completely off guard as Oscar's jaws clenched down upon his spindly arm. Isaac managed to break free and swim to the safety of the ceramic sunken pirate ship in the center of the tank, while Oscar made off with a bony little snack. Although the incident had long passed, and Oscar apologized several times, Isaac never forgave the fish, and to this day, doesn't let down his guard in Oscar's presence. Both held senior management positions at SCRAPPI, though Rae Zorr, the piranha CEO, knew enough to keep them separated whenever possible.

The PI Gear line was coming together nicely. The shoes and clothes had been designed, but there was still a need to fine-tune the colors and patterns to best accentuate the other design elements. For this job, Isaac instructed Jerry to recruit a temperamental, yet talented pot-bellied pig named Vincent. Vincent was a master designer, an artiste extraordinaire, having held previous positions with the likes of Calvin Swine and L.L. Barn.

Vincent worked out of an office several hundred miles away, however, so Jerry would have to communicate with him through phone, fax, and e-mail, as face-to-face meetings would be difficult to arrange. This didn't bother Jerry though; he particularly enjoyed using e-mail, finding it to be a quick and efficient means of communication.

Isaac instructed Jerry to contact the artist, describe the PI Gear project, and request his participation.

"He's brilliant. We really need his genius to succeed with this one. We'll have to watch our spending, but be sure to tell him we can offer whatever support he might need."

Jerry first attempted to contact Vincent by phone, but was directed to his voice mailbox. Jerry would be in and out of his own office for the next several days, and did not wish to engage Vincent in an endless round of phone tag, so he opted not to leave a message. Jerry also considered contacting Vincent by letter, but chose e-mail instead. This would allow him to communicate in a more timely fashion, and would be a lot easier than writing letters, as errors in capitalization, grammar, spelling, and word choice are more readily accepted in e-mail than in letters and memos. Jerry sat down at his computer and typed the following message to the pig, Vincent:

<<hello vincent. my nam e is jerry mulligan. i work over at corprate offices. need your hlep on new product line called pig ear. when i asked you're old fiend isaac who he'd recommmend for the job—he said you were dead. ringer. product line promises to do quiet well. could use your head on this one. let me know. thanks.

j.>>

Like most of us, Jerry's e-mail messages were not very polished, and he tended to whip them off quickly. They were short, to the point, and only rarely proofread before sent. For some reason, there were certain typing errors he made repeatedly, like misspelling "help" and goofing up the spacing on "pi gear."

Vincent had taken the morning off to do some painting with two friends, both swine, from his art club. One pig, Casso, specialized in cubist sculptures and paintings. The other, Andy Warthog, preferred pop art paintings and film. Vincent was an impressionist, and was currently working on a self-portrait.

Vincent's morning had not gone well. A month earlier, he completed a painting of which he was particularly proud. It was a nostalgic piece, a still life depicting Vincent's first love—a 1966 VW van. He titled it "Vincent's Van." Vincent's fellow artists liked the painting so much they voted to display it in the foyer of the studio. Well, when Vincent and his two friends entered the studio that morning, "Vincent's Van" was missing! The three porcine painters searched high and low for the masterpiece, but it was nowhere to be found. The question on everyone's mind was, "Where did 'Vincent's Van' go?" Disheartening as it was, the trio concluded it must have been stolen. Andy Warthog and the pig, Casso, tried to console their friend, but to no avail.

This sort of thing had happened at the three little pigs' previous studios, but those buildings were easy to break into, having been constructed of straw and sticks, respectively. The new studio was made of brick, and was considered impervious to intruders. Vincent was devastated. Could his day possibly get any worse?

When he returned to his desk that afternoon, Vincent saw Jerry's message and opened it.

"What's this?" he thought to himself, "A new product line called *pig ear!!?* Isaac wants me *dead*?! They want to use *my head*??!"

By this point, Vincent was in the throes of a full-fledged conniption. Like many artists, Vincent's creativity and expressiveness were fueled by a deep sense of emotion. His feelings were hard to control, however, and his mood swings were sometimes severe. The company had asked a lot of him over the years, but he couldn't believe they expected him to give up his own ears! Vincent chuckled momentarily as he imagined his self-portrait sans ears, but then quickly shifted back to an emotional state of shock. Even if SCRAPPI was producing pig ear products, company policy dictated no animals would be assigned to work on products made from their own species, much less their very own body parts! This policy had been in effect since 1982, when a horse who worked in the food processing plant had a nervous breakdown after realizing his grandmother was a key ingredient in the batch of "Scrappi Senior Blend" (specially formulated for older dogs) that he'd just mixed.

Why would Sir Isaac the newt choose him for this? Who was this Jerry Mulligan? And even if Vincent did have to give up his ears, why would they have to decapitate him? Surely they could have removed them surgically, without necessitating his demise. Perhaps he misunderstood Jerry's message.

Vincent collected himself and wrote his reply:

<<mr. mulligan. not sure i understand what you want from me. sure you need my head for this thing? please clarify expectations.

vincent>>

When Jerry received Vincent's reply, he realized he failed to specify his desire for the pig to help with color selection for the fabric-dyeing process. He needed Vincent's talents to ensure the PI Gear looked its best. Jerry wrote back:

> <<sorry for the co nfusiun. isaac said you'd have right stuff to help make pig ear line successsful. he said that without your head we'd nevr be able to make it. we're alreaddy over budget, so looking for ways to keep things simple and econommical. need to make sure we make cuts in right places. need input on your preference for dying process. of course, you can let us know of any assistace you migt need. We want to make this as painless as possible for you.
>
> j.>>

Jerry was sure this would clear things up. Of course, when Vincent received Jerry's message, he didn't exactly read it the way Jerry intended. He still couldn't believe Jerry's insistence on having him killed. Sure, it might be more cost-effective to overnight his dismembered corpse to the corporate offices rather than purchase a plane ticket, but certainly the company didn't have to be *that* cutthroat!…nor that thrifty. Vincent wrote back:

> <<jerry. i find this whole project to be very disturbing. dying may not be necessary. i think we can make cuts in right places and still come up with compromise we can all live with. i've given a lot to this company, but i have to draw the line somewhere.>>

"Wow," thought Jerry. "He's really overreacting! Sir Isaac wasn't kidding when he warned me about Vincent's temperament! I guess I'm going to have to find someone else to help me. I'll try to be as pleasant as I can—I don't want to make enemies over this."

So, Jerry wrote back:

> <<fine. will look for anothher volunter. any suggestions?
>
> j.>>

"The *nerve* of this guy!" thought Vincent. "*Fine*?! How dare he take that obnoxious tone with me!" He wrote back:

<<mr. mulligan. you are obviously scum of the earth. what kind of pig do you think i am? i would never turn over one of my friends to help you with your sick little project. company e-mail policy prohibits me from writing what i really think of you. though you may not have my whole head, i hope to meet you some day, so i can at least give you a piece of my mind.>>

Jerry didn't quite know what to make of this, but knew he must have fouled up somehow. He needed Sophia's help...right away. So he summoned her with his magic dog whistle.

Sophia appeared. The two caught up on each other's families and such. Then Jerry showed Sophia the string of e-mails, and she quickly surmised what had happened.

"You're really not much of a typist, are you Jerry? And where did you learn to spell? I can't imagine you send formal letters looking like that."

"What's the big deal? It's only internal e-mail."

"Look, Jerry. E-mail is great, but you've got to be careful with it. Those kinds of brief and truncated messages are fine with folks you deal with every day, but they can lead to huge misunderstandings with those less familiar with your style. You've never met this pig, Vincent, right?"

"No, I've never even spoken with him."

"I'm not sure e-mail was the best mode for making an initial contact here. For someone you are inviting to work with you, it's probably best to take a more personal approach, like a face-to-face meeting, or a phone call if the face-to-face is not feasible. You'll do a better job of communicating effectively and putting others at ease when they can experience your facial expressions and body language, or at least your tone of voice. Folks have a tendency to read harsh tones into the written word. E-mail is even more susceptible to this problem than formal letters, because with the latter, it's generally expected the writer will take some time to set a pleasant tone and provide sufficient background and context."

"Well, I did try calling him first," Jerry said in a defensive tone. "But I didn't want him calling me back when I was in the middle of something else, or when I might not be prepared to talk with him. E-mail just seemed a lot more practical."

> # Choose your mode of communication carefully. Use technology, but don't hide behind it.

"Jerry, look at your first message carefully. Did you notice how you spaced PI Gear? You made the same mistake twice. I have a similar habit in that when I type quickly, I usually spell the word 'thanks' 'T-H-N-A-K-S.' I have to double check it each time I send a message."

"Let me see that. Oops!" Jerry's eyes suddenly widened as he realized the implications of his simple spacing error.

"No wonder Vincent was so testy with me. He must have thought I wanted to chop his ears off and make some new product out of them!"

"And look how you spelled 'dyeing.'"

"Isn't that how it's spelled?"

"Well, if you're talking about a dying breed, but not if you're talking about a dyeing process. Even a spell checker wouldn't have covered that one for you. Every once in a while, you still need to look things up, Techno-Boy. Didn't you proof this at *all*?"

"Uh-oh. This is worse than I thought," muttered Jerry.

"You were in such a rush to fire off your message, in the interest of saving time, you created more time-consuming work for yourself in the long run."

> # Slow down enough to communicate with precision.

"I have to give you credit for one thing, Mulligan. A lesser dog might have sent off an angry response to Vincent's final message."

"My first instinct was to attack."

"What held you back?"

"Experience. I've stuck my paw in my mouth so many times when I was emotionally wrapped up in a situation. I knew I'd regret it if I did that again."

"Yeah, don't open your mouth until you can regulate your emotions."

> # It is generally best to address misunderstandings as soon as possible. But if you are angry, be sure to cool down first.

Jerry continued, "You know, Sophia, I think if you turn the clock back now, I can finish this one on my own."

"I think so too, Jerry."

"Thanks again for your help. You're a life saver."

Jerry made a few adjustments in his approach to Vincent. And Vincent responded quite well. Also, in the course of their conversations, Jerry learned of Vincent's stolen painting. And having developed a fondness for the pig, Jerry enlisted Sophia in turning back time a few days before their initial contact so he could recommend Vincent remove his painting from the studio before it was stolen. (Though the identity of the big bad thief is not important, let's just say it's no coincidence that VWs are manufactured in *Wolfs*burg.) No longer would others wonder where "Vincent's Van" had gone. Instead, the buzz in the amateur art community was, "How far will 'Vincent's Van' Gogh?"

In the end, Jerry's team was responsible for getting PI Gear to market three months ahead of schedule! Jerry Mulligan's star was definitely on the rise. In fact, Vincent was so inspired by his impressive canine friend from Carson Ridge, he titled his next painting, "Starry Knight," in Jerry's honor.

Mulligan's Mull-Agains

1. Keeping both efficiency and effectiveness in mind, which mode should I use to communicate my message?

2. Am I being careful enough with what I write to ensure that my implicit tone and meaning cannot be misunderstood?

3. Would I choose softer words if I were communicating face-to-face?

4. If things are getting emotional, how can I tone down my own intensity so we can stay focused on constructively solving the problem?

5. I wonder if I could get Vincent to paint a pigture of me.

5

Fast Track to the Top

It was a typical early autumn day about 7 a.m. Jerry wandered onto the deck in his backyard, downing his last swallow of coffee, and taking satisfaction as he surveyed the quarter acre of suburbia he'd worked so hard to acquire. He noticed a light frost covering the shaded portion of his lawn…as yet undiscovered by the warming rays of morning sunshine. His tail wagged involuntarily, rhythmically nipping the periphery of his field of vision…left…then right…left…then right. He thought of Gertrude and the children. They had little more than each other. Yet somehow, Jerry could not have been happier if he were the richest dog in the world. Life was good.

The commute to the office was uneventful that day. Jerry was still grieving the loss of those five extra minutes of sleep he had enjoyed every day during the summer. Now that the school buses were running again, there were a lot more stops and starts along the route, so Jerry had to allow more time to get to work. But by now, he was getting used to it.

Jerry pulled into the lot, barked his car, fetched his briefcase from the trunk, and made his way into the building. His cubicle was one of nearly two hundred that had been grouped together in a maze-like configuration in the center of the third floor, an area the employees referred to as "the kennel." As Jerry neared his workspace, he noticed a small cluster of helium balloons tied to his office chair. There was also a card and a flowering potted plant. Jerry slowly opened the envelope, as he wondered what might have occasioned the unexpected gift.

The card was from the CEO, Rae Zorr. And while the fin-writing was a bit difficult to decipher, the message was clear. Jerry Mulligan received a huge promotion, effective immediately!

He would be SCRAPPI's Director of Operations for its dynamic new product line, Therapetz. What an opportunity! Therapetz was definitely cutting edge.

You see, like their human owners, household pets everywhere were succumbing to the stress, anxiety, and worry of an increasingly fast-paced world. And new technologies, despite their promise of making life easier and more comfortable, yielded little more than increased complexity and lengthier "to do" lists.

Now, for the first time in history, there would be a major push to help household pets cope with their difficult lives. Therapetz was a full line of stress management products designed to do just that...and Jerry Mulligan would lead the way.

Jerry would oversee operations and production for the entire division. More than eight hundred and fifty employees in all! This was a tough assignment. Not just because of the obvious disadvantages of being the only animal-run company in the world, nor because of the workforce diversity issues (imagine snakes and cats sharing the plant floor with mice and goldfish! Talk about a management challenge!). SCRAPPI always had more than its share of the backbiting, cat fighting, and predatory predilections common to corporate America. But Jerry would have a chance to change all of that, at least as far as his little corner of the world was concerned. He envisioned teamwork, productivity, and results. He had the new watch, the clothes, and now, the title. But Jerry Mulligan would now be tested like never before. Could *he* do the job?

By this time, SCRAPPI had the largest market share of pet products in the industry. Multinational, with nine manufacturing plants, forty-eight distribution centers, twenty-two thousand employees, and annual revenues in excess of $4.3 billion, SCRAPPI was a force to be reckoned with.

The pressure was on. Jerry had to do this right or face the consequences. As far as Therapetz was concerned, the buck would stop at Jerry's desk. He was just two steps removed from Ms. Zorr, with only Mitch Shellhouser, a hermit crab, between them. Mitch was the Chief Operations Officer, somewhat of an enigma, as he loved to get out on the plant floor and mix with the employees. He was gruff and demanding, but very well-liked.

And then there was Jerry's Administrative Assistant, Flora, a capable and well-meaning Venus flytrap. She was delicate and attractive, and though she was the only plant at the plant, she had strong animal instincts. Flora never got out of her chair, yet no one could accuse her of laziness. She was organized to the hilt, with a reputation for effectiveness and efficiency.

Despite a severe case of the jitters (not to mention mild cases of eczema and canine halitosis), Jerry had to appear calm and confident. He knew many of the others questioned his competence. He questioned it himself. Did management really know what they were doing when they offered him the promotion? Sure, he had done well, even excelled in prior roles. But this was a whole new ball game (not just a simple game of "fetch"). This time, it wasn't about designing and building *products*. It was about designing and building an entire division. And for this job, Jerry had to develop the same mastery with relationships that he had with machinery and operational processes. Not that he had to become the next Dogter Laura, but he had to be good enough to create, maintain, and lead a high-performing team, which requires *relational* strength. Could he pull it off? Time would tell.

Jerry's conscience was strong. He always tried to do what was best. He understood as a leader, he would be challenged to balance his responsibilities to both the company and his workers. The workers must perform at their best in order for the company to prosper in a competitive environment. And yet, the company must also perform at its best in order for the workers to prosper. He truly believed what's best for the company is best for the employees, and vice versa.

Therapetz' last Director of Operations didn't last very long, only about fourteen months. She was the one who got the entire project up and running, but because of "philosophical differences" with Mr. Shellhouser, she was forced to leave. So by the time of Jerry's arrival on the scene, the Therapetz division was operational, but had thus far gained little momentum.

Jerry wasted no time getting to work. His new digs were much nicer than "the kennel." Now Jerry had windows, a door, a large desk, and even a private washroom equipped with a sink, shower, and fire hydrant. He would add a few personal items, like pictures of Gertrude and the children, some motivational posters, and a golf putting practice mat.

Jerry had moved in during the weekend to organize his office, and scheduled an early morning meeting with both Mitch Shellhouser and Bud Green. Bud was an iguana. Though his skin was green, he certainly was not. In fact, Bud was among the most seasoned workers Jerry had on his team. Word had it Bud knew his stuff, but was a bit two-faced. As a middle manager, he played the "us versus them" game so adeptly his subordinates jokingly referred to him as "The chameleon" (a close cousin to the iguana); changing colors depending on which crowd he wished to blend with.

Bud was the production supervisor for a new item called Squeezers Stress Relievers. Squeezers would be billed as the ultimate in tension relief. They looked just like a racquetball. They were round and, well, squishy—made with a durable rubber cover encasing a pliable putty core. A stressed-out house pet could obtain rapid relief from muscle tension by alternately tightening and loosening their grip on these flexible rubber novelties.

Squeezers were about to go into production. Just a few decisions remained before they were a "go." Research and Development was working to find just the right durability-to-squishiness ratio. The idea was to make the product durable enough to stand up to heavy use, yet mushy enough to allow maximum tension relief. A more durable cover would result in a more firm, and thus less effective Squeezer. Yet manufacturing a more squishy Squeezer required thinning the cover, which could only be accomplished at the expense of durability. R&D needed direction. The final decision belonged to Jerry.

Jerry wanted to impress his boss. He also wanted Bud the iguana to respect his decisiveness. But at this point, he had no idea what to do. So he asked Bud to summon someone from the R&D team. Jerry would ask a few questions and ascertain the best course of action.

Bud didn't think much of R&D. To him, they seemed out of touch with reality. They played with their little inventions, but weren't very practical.

"Look Jerry, I can tell you now we'll need to go with durability. Those eggheads aren't going to tell you anything new. Trust me on this."

Jerry was annoyed Bud would challenge him so openly his first day on the job. And in front of Mr. Shellhouser!

"Bud, just get someone from R&D in here."

Bud disappeared for a few moments while Mitch made small talk. He asked Jerry about his family, hobbies, aspirations and such. Jerry was flattered by Mitch's interest, and obliged him with sophisticated and lengthy answers designed to showcase his own "depth" and personal complexity. Jerry felt good he handled himself so well and made the most of this opportunity to make a positive impression. It occurred to him though, that in fifteen minutes of discussion, he hadn't learned one new thing about Mitch.

"Excuse me." Bud returned with someone from R&D. Dr. Goodfur was a domesticated snowshoe hare who had studied both chemistry and physics at the Alaskan Institute of Technology. She was absolutely brilliant and was the leader of the R&D team. After introductions, Jerry got to the point.

"So, Dr. Goodfur, I understand we're having a little trouble finding just the right SD ratio." (By 'SD' Jerry was referring to the squishiness-to-durability ratio, but he thought it would improve his credibility if he could use acronyms and jargon.)

"That's correct," Dr. Goodfur responded. "If we want durability, we'll have to sacrifice squishiness, and thus potentially diminish the stress-reducing effectiveness of the product."

Bud chimed in. "If those things tear apart after only a few months' use, we'll get a reputation for poor quality. I don't want that on *my* head!"

Mitch added, "But our reputation is at stake. If our products don't do what we say they'll do…if these things won't actually relax anybody, then we'll be the laughing stock of the annual Pet Products Trade Show next month in Albuquerque. Make sure they're soft enough to work!"

"There's more to consider here," said Dr. Goodfur. "For example, the customer. We need to get a better sense of how the Squeezers will be used, and who will…"

"Good point, Goodfur," Jerry interrupted. "We'll need to exceed customer expectations. If those monkeys are expecting stress relief, let's be sure to relieve their stress more than they ever dreamed possible!"

"Well, I'm not sure the monkeys are the ones we should be most…"

"Dr. Goodfur," Jerry interrupted again, "We must become more customer-focused. Exceeding customer expectations must be the philosophy that guides everything we do with Therapetz! We will never survive in this competitive environment if we ignore customer needs. Give the customers what they want. Give them more than what they expect! Dr. Goodfur, can you make the Squeezers squishier?"

"Well, yes, but…"

"Great! Then it's settled. Increase the SD ratio to 1.57. Are you okay with that, Bud?"

"Sure, but if the covers wear out too soon, I don't want to hear about it."

Dr. Goodfur was obviously getting annoyed. The fur along her shoulders began to stand up. Her nose began to twitch, and her eyes narrowed. This time, she got a little snippy.

"Look, I think 1.57 is a bit high."

"Well," Jerry responded, "What ratio do they typically use when they make these things for humans?"

"1.6, but that doesn't necessarily mean…"

"1.6!? Well, then 1.57 is too *low*. Pets need to relax every bit as much as humans do. Raise the ratio to 1.6. And let's shoot to have them ready by the sixth of the month. Is that do-able?"

Dr. Goodfur said with a defeated sigh, "Sure. By the way, we're going to need some help with the raw materials. They ship the putty in fifty-five gallon drums. It tends to harden after sitting a while. We can thin it out eventually, but the putty scoops aren't working very well. Can you free up someone from the production floor to help us out?"

Jerry replied, "Why don't you just use a spade?"

"A spayed?" Goodfur asked, incensed Jerry would use such a derogatory term for a cat that had been 'fixed.' (This was the equivalent of a human referring to someone as a 'broad' or 'chick.' She didn't realize he was referring to a small shovel with a sharp edge.)

Well, Jerry had certainly made no friend out of Dr. Goodfur. His first day on the job, he'd managed to impress his immediate boss, or so he thought. But he also alienated two other key players.

The rest of the week was relatively uneventful. There were the usual meetings, tours, and training that are part of any new job. The sixth day of the month eventually rolled around. R&D came through on schedule. They put together a batch of prototype Squeezers and began test marketing.

After returning from lunch two days later, Jerry checked his voice mail. There was an angry message from Mitch Shellhouser.

"I hear there were some *major* problems with the Squeezers. This one is going to be costly. I'll be at your office at four o'clock today. Rae Zorr will be coming with me. Make sure you're available! Tails will droop!" (This was the equivalent of saying 'heads will roll' in a human-run organization.)

Jerry had made a colossal mistake. But what could it have been? He was afraid to call Mitch. Then he would really look bad. He nervously paced his office, like a caged beast, racking his brains. He envisioned himself getting fired…blacklisted…never to find work again. He and his family out on the streets, rummaging through trash cans for food. He needed Sophia NOW!

The minute Sophia arrived, the panic-stricken Irish setter was all over her.

"Mitch Shellhouser and Rae Zorr are coming over this afternoon to chew me out. That's about all I know. You've got to help me!"

Sophia patiently listened to Jerry's nervous ranter until his energy was spent. "You know the drill," she said. "Let's get started. I'm going to take you back to that first day in your new position. Let's look at what happened. Here we go!"

Back in time, to the meeting with Mitch and Bud: Jerry asked Bud to bring in the R&D people, and Bud responded with, "Look Jerry, I can tell you now that we're going to need to go with durability. Those eggheads aren't going to tell you anything new. Trust me on this."

Sophia began, "Jerry, who do you think has the most control over whether communication occurs? The speaker, or the listener?"

"I never really thought about it." He paused a moment to reflect. "The speaker, I guess."

"Actually, no. You see, no matter how much the speaker has to say, communication cannot occur unless the listener is receiving the message."

A good communicator is first and foremost a good listener.

"Jerry, you're not a very good listener. You are in trouble today because you failed to communicate on that first day. Sure, you had a lot to say, but you missed much of what Bud, Mitch, and Dr. Goodfur had to offer. You misread them, and you failed to obtain critical information that could have helped you solve the Squeezer dilemma more effectively. In other words, you created your own mess."

"I still don't see what the mess is!"

"Be patient, you will. Let's get back to listening skills. Jerry, how can you tell when someone is listening attentively to you? When they're

really in tune with what you're trying to convey? What do they do that demonstrates they're trying to receive your message?"

"Well, they usually face me with their body and look me in the eye."

"What else do you notice about their body language?"

"They might lean forward, and their posture and facial expressions seem to show a certain reactivity to my words. Like if I say something funny, they'll smile. Or if I say something puzzling, they might sit back and get a perplexed look on their face. They might also nod to indicate their understanding, or shake their head to signal disagreement."

"Now you're getting it. What about verbal cues?"

"I suppose an occasional 'hmm' or 'uh-huh' helps. Also, if they ask relevant questions or summarize what I've told them, then I can be pretty sure that they're getting it."

"That's good, Jerry. Now tell me how you feel, by contrast, when someone is not listening."

"How I *feel?* Well, I start feeling devalued…like what I say doesn't really matter. And that makes me annoyed and even angry sometimes."

"Now tell me how you can sense when someone is not really listening. What do they say or do that conveys a lack of interest or lack of respect for your opinions?"

"Hmm. They might divide their attention between me and something else. For example, they might be reading something while I'm trying to talk to them, or they may be facing another direction. Or they'll just keep giving me their ideas without even responding to mine. I remember a meeting I had with Ms. Zorr last week. She seemed distracted. Even asked me the same question twice, like she never heard the first time I answered it. She covered it quickly with a, 'Oh, that's right. You did say that.' But I'll tell you, when I walked out of there, I felt like she didn't give a rip about one word I said."

"Jerry, I know it may not feel this way to you, but you have a tendency to bowl people over."

"Me?"

"Absolutely. Not in an overtly aggressive way, but in a way that conveys a certain arrogance, self-absorption, and disregard for others."

"Ouch! Do I really do all that?"

"That day of the meeting, you brushed aside Bud's opinion, talked only about yourself with Mitch, and interrupted Dr. Goodfur every time she tried to get a word in edgewise. You need all of these folks on board in order to do your job, yet you managed to alienate each one of them on your first day. You set a tone of tension and conflict rather than cooperation."

"Well, Bud's a difficult creature. Everybody knows that. He didn't want R&D involved at all. I knew they needed to be. I couldn't just dismiss their input simply because Bud doesn't respect them."

"Agreed. But it would help to show that you understand and respect his position before deciding to overrule him. I want you to remember something important:

> # The first step toward taking someone with you is to meet them where they are.

"You mean I have to do my best to understand where they're coming from before worrying about whether or not they understand or agree with me?"

"Exactly. When you show people you are genuinely interested in what they think and what's important to them, you communicate that you value and respect them. And someone who feels valued and respected is more likely to give you their best, and to show value and respect toward you."

Effective listening promotes a tone of cooperation.

"One other thing," added Sophia. *"When you're involved in an important interaction, take notes. Doing so communicates that the information you are exchanging is important to you. Taking notes will also help you to reconstruct the interaction accurately, especially if there is a time lag between the meeting and the follow-up actions that you or others must undertake. Finally, you can tactfully double-check you are 'receiving' accurately by saying something like, 'Okay, I've written _____. Do I have that right?'"*

When you need to get it right, write it down.

"So, Jerry, are you ready to try this one again?"
"I think so. Let's do it."

Jerry began his response to Bud, keeping in mind his discussion with Sophia.

"I trust your judgment, Bud. I know your reputation, and I am counting on you to contribute your expertise from a production standpoint. But I would like input from R&D also. We've got the best chance of coming up with the most workable plan if we hear from all the major players."

Then, leaning forward, Jerry added, "I really don't know anyone on the R&D team. Who do you think should join us?"

"I don't know. They're all a little quirky," replied Bud.

"Well, which one do you think could offer the most useful perspective?"

"Probably Dr. Goodfur the hare. She's usually pretty reasonable."

"That sounds good. Would you mind tracking her down and inviting her here?"

"Sure."

"Thanks, Bud."

"Nice job, Jerry," said Sophia. "You're getting the hang of this. Now remember: when you talk to Mitch Shellhouser, put a muzzle on, and let your ears do some of the work!"

Like the first time through, Mitch initiated the small talk once Bud left. But this time, Jerry worried less about showcasing himself, and focused instead on learning more about Mitch. After all, if he was going to work with Mitch, it might be worthwhile to find out what makes Mitch tick. Jerry learned Mitch enjoys the beach, and has a condominium in the very town where Jerry used to vacation with his family as a pup. He also discovered they both like to play golf, and Mitch values punctuality. Jerry took note of this, figuring it would be wise to be a few minutes early to meetings with Mitch.

"Excuse me." Bud returned with Dr. Goodfur. After introductions, Jerry asked Dr. Goodfur a few questions about her work for SCRAPPI and then got to the point.

"So, Dr. Goodfur, I understand we're having a little trouble finding just the right squishiness-to-durability ratio."

"That's correct. If we want durability, we'll have to sacrifice squishiness, and thus potentially diminish the stress-reducing effectiveness of the product."

Bud chimed in, "If those things tear apart after only a few months' use, we'll get a reputation for poor quality. I don't want that on *my* head!"

Mitch added, "But our reputation is at stake. If our products don't do what we say they'll do…if these things won't actually relax anybody, then we'll be the laughing stock of the trade show. Make sure they're soft enough to work!"

Jerry responded, "Bud, you raise a good point about the importance of durability. And Mitch, I'd agree our products must do what we say they'll do. I think we can all agree if we miss the SD ratio in *either* direction, we've got trouble."

"Good summary, Jerry. That's a nice way of keeping focus on the team's goal."

"There's more to consider here," said Dr. Goodfur. "For example, the customer. We need to get a better sense of how the Squeezers will be used, and who will be using them."

Jerry responded, "I assume the monkeys will be using them the same way the humans do; simply squeezing them in the palms of their hands…or feet, as the case may be. In any event, we should be fairly safe with design specifications that have proven best for humans."

"Well, I'm not sure the monkeys are the ones we should be most concerned about," said Goodfur. "In fact, I was under the impression our target market would be dogs who suffer from TMJ."

"Dogs with TMJ!?" bellowed Jerry, Mitch, and Bud in unison.

"Yes. Didn't any of you read the marketing report? With so few people actually keeping monkeys as pets, we don't stand to make much by targeting primates. But there are dogs in thirty-five percent of all households, and TMJ is a common canine affliction. Dogs benefit by *chewing* on Squeezers, not squeezing them in their paws. If we match the human specs with a relatively high SD ratio, dogs will chew through the covers after the first few uses. If we want them to last, on the other hand, we'll need to make the covers more durable."

"You're doing much better with the interruptions this time, Jerry," added Sophia. *"See what you can learn when you just let others say their piece."*

"I see your point," Jerry said to Dr. Goodfur. "What SD ratio would you recommend for dogs?"

"Somewhere between 0.7 and 0.8 would be ideal."

"That sounds about right to me," added Bud. "Hey, Doc, do you think you might be able to flavor the covers? That will go over big with dogs."

"I think we can manage that," said Dr. Goodfur. "Jerry, you're a dog. What flavors would you like to see?"

"My favorites are lamb & rice, door post, and old slipper."

"Why don't you add *mint* to the list," said Mitch with a snicker. Bud and Dr. Goodfur chuckled along, as they all knew a few dogs who could stand to be more attentive to oral hygiene. Jerry could see there was no harm intended, and knew there was a grain of truth to their words, so he chortled along with them.

Dr. Goodfur continued, "Looks like we've got the cover figured out. I'm going to need some help with the putty we use to make the core. It's shipped in fifty-five gallon drums. It tends to harden after sitting a while. We can thin it out eventually, but it's going slow, and we're breaking a lot of putty scoops in the meantime. Can you free up someone from Production to help us out?"

Jerry replied, "Why don't you just use a spade?"

"A spayed?" Goodfur asked, again thinking Jerry was referring to a cat.

"You look puzzled. Am I being unclear?"

"Not really. I'm just kind of shocked you would refer to one of our workers in such a derogatory way," said Dr. Goodfur.

"Heavens, no! I mean a *spade*…S-P-A-D-E! You know, a little shovel with a sharp edge."

"Ohhh!" They all laughed at their little misunderstanding. They agreed on a date to begin production and ended the meeting.

Back to the present, the eighth of the month. Jerry and Sophia continued their discussion in the privacy of Jerry's office.

"Well, Jerry, things certainly seem to have worked out better this time. Wouldn't you agree?"

"I'll say! What a disaster I created! No wonder Mitch was so upset with me! My earlier decision to set the SD ratio so high was based on a false assumption that Squeezers would be for primates only. Once the dogs got a hold of the prototypes with their teeth, we must have been blowing covers left and right!"

"Do you see what I meant when I said you had created your own mess?"

"I sure do. And what about Dr. Goodfur and that shovel? I can't believe she thought I was referring to a sterilized cat? No wonder she reacted so strongly."

"Yes, Jerry, that certainly illustrates the importance of checking to see that your message is understood as intended."

"So, does this mean everything is okay?…and Mitch won't be coming over this afternoon to chew me out?"

"I don't know. Your voice mail light is flashing. Why don't you see for yourself."

Jerry pressed the "VM" button on his phone. It was Mitch all right. But this time his tone was much different.

"Jerry, great job on the Squeezers! Consumer testing seems to be going well. The dogs love them! Rae wants to congratulate you personally, so she and I will be stopping by around four o'clock. I'll have some Squeezer samples dropped off at your place before the meeting so you can try them out yourself. Might I suggest you start with door post or slipper, and go with mint or cinnamon as a chaser? See you then."

"Wow! What a difference! I had no idea what I was missing by not listening well."

Good listening facilitates the right results.

Mulligan's Mull-Agains

1. Am I authentic in my interactions with others, or am I trying too hard to impress them?

2. Am I careful to really listen to what others have to say?

3. Do I tend to interrupt others? (Maybe I should ask others for their opinion on this.)

4. What efforts can I make to show interest and better understand others' positions before imposing my position on them?

5. How can I check to see my messages are properly understood?

6. If Mitch Shellhouser weren't a hermit crab, would he still clamor for a bigger office each year?

6

The Chips are Down

Several months passed since Jerry Mulligan's latest mulligan. He adjusted nicely to the new job. He thought of Sophia often, and regularly practiced his newfound listening skills. Sometimes, as a means of guidance, Jerry would ask himself, "I wonder how Sophia would handle this situation?"

Over the same time period, the Dow Jones took quite a beating. Consumer confidence was low. Likewise, SCRAPPI had hit rough seas. Interestingly, when the economy slows and consumer spending declines, one of the first items slashed from most family budgets is pet supplies. To the dismay of SCRAPPI, humans take better care of their own kind than they do of their pets (though there are exceptions). Pet owners were downgrading from premium feed to those generic grocery store "econo-bulk-bags." Toys and other perks were eliminated altogether. And any gerbil who dared to dream of getting that new addition to the habitrail had another thing coming!

The slowdown made things a bit tense at SCRAPPI. Jerry felt it was important for everyone to know the seriousness of the situation, yet he did not want to create a sense of panic. Walking that fine line was challenging. A hiring freeze was on, and spending on non-essentials was strictly forbidden. Of course, there were rumors of layoffs and shutdowns, but so far, Jerry's division had avoided such extreme measures. Nonetheless, some hard decisions had to be made, and Jerry would have to make them.

Despite low consumer demand and reduced production, Jerry was as busy as ever, perhaps even more so. It seemed he was putting fires out everywhere, barely finding time to manage the crises, much less plan ahead.

The Accounting Department was headed by Rick Feasel, a ferret with a reputation for doing whatever it took to protect the company's interests. Needless to say, he was not a favorite among the production workers (who referred to him as "Slick Weasel"), but management valued his talent. He wore thick glasses and drank way too much coffee. He was accustomed to putting in long hours, which left him a bit high-strung. But he always seemed to get the job done.

Rick and Jerry had been spending lots of time together lately, poring over budgets, desperately looking for ways to cut costs and improve cash flow. Fortunately, the Therapetz line was not suffering as badly as other divisions. With the stress accompanying the economic downturn, sales for SCRAPPI's stress reduction pet products could have been worse. Squeezers were still selling well. With luck, Therapetz would weather the crisis without layoffs.

One target of the budget cuts was the cedar chips used in employee restrooms. Cedar was expensive, and the chips had to be replaced several times a day. Eliminating the cedar chips would reduce the cost of janitorial services, which were outsourced anyway, and would also positively impact insurance premiums, as the chips posed a fire hazard. Nonetheless, Jerry suspected this decision would not go well with the gerbils, rats, hamsters, and guinea pigs. As part of a company-wide effort to improve morale, the chips had been added a few months earlier at the suggestion of a mouse named "Stinky."

Jerry dreaded announcing the change. He knew that seemingly small conveniences—like restroom amenities, snack carts, picnic

tables, bottled water, and the like—can be important to employees, and eliminating them can harm morale. Jerry considered
delivering the message personally, perhaps by calling a special
meeting with the workers. But as he envisioned himself bombarded with questions and accusations from an angry group, Jerry
opted for avoidance instead. He already had enough crises to
manage, and the last thing he needed was another headache.

The decision was made. Jerry would see to it the cedar chips
were removed before the morning shift arrived the next day. He
asked Rick to notify the employees.

"Will do," said Rick.

The next morning, a sign appeared in each of the employee
restrooms:

Due to the current financial
crisis, there will be no more
cedar chips in the restrooms.

—The Management

Stinky, who was one of the more conscientious workers, was the
first to punch in that day, and having suffered from a compulsive
paw-washing disorder, was also the first to use the restroom. He
knew right away something was amiss, as the restroom did not
have its usual cedar aroma. Then, when he saw Rick's sign (which
he assumed had been posted at Jerry's direction), Stinky reacted in
anger and fear.

"What could this mean?" he thought. "I knew things were tight,
but *'crisis?'* Why are they targeting *us*, the small rodents? What's
next? Are they planning to lay us off? I'd better tell the others."

Predictably, the plant floor was abuzz with panic. Rumors were flying everywhere. Fearful and angry, the workers retaliated in the only way they knew…low productivity, lengthy breaks, and high defect rates.

Jerry didn't arrive until afternoon, as he had been off-site for a series of meetings. On the way toward his office, he could feel the cold reception. His usual cheery greetings were met with uncharacteristic grunts and restrained mutterings. From the doorknob of his office dangled a pooper-scooper with a sticky note that read:

```
So nice of you to dump on us.

                              —The Peons
```

Uh-oh, this was not good! Jerry summoned Flora, his Venus flytrap assistant, having momentarily forgotten that, as a potted plant, she didn't move around much. So, Jerry went to her office instead. Flora always seemed to know what was going on. She had a special informant of sorts…a regular "fly on the wall" named Ucho. Flora had once captured Ucho for a snack, but the quick-thinking insect struck a deal to spare his life. He would eavesdrop for Flora if she would let him live. Ironically, "Ucho" is a Czech word that means "ear."

Flora told Jerry what happened. Jerry knew what had to be done. He reached for the magic dog whistle and gave it a blow as he thought to himself, "Sophia, I need you…now!"

"Jerry, how are you? It's been so long."

"Well, I've been better."

As she read the note on Jerry's doorknob, Sophia said, "Apparently so. What happened?"

Jerry filled her in on the situation.

"Boy, Jerry, it sounds like things have been pretty rough around here lately."

"They sure have. Everybody's a bit edgy. I feel so awful. I could kick myself for sending Rick to notify the employees about the cedar chips. I should have done that myself."

"Yeah, that doesn't sound like delegation to me. Seems more like avoidance. Why didn't you make the announcement yourself?"

"I've been so tired of the negativity around this place lately. I just dreaded telling them we would be taking away one more thing. I pictured all the disappointment and questions and grumbling, which I knew they would direct right at me…I really didn't want to deal with it."

"But look at what you're dealing with *now* instead. Mulligan, I don't know anyone who enjoys delivering a hard message. It's canine nature to avoid such things. It sounds like you looked at what was right in front of you—the pain of facing that crowd—but you never stepped back long enough to consider the longer-term consequences of *not* facing the employees. You chose to do what was *easiest* in the short run over what was *best* in the long run.

> # Communicating takes time and energy. But doing so clearly, and up front, almost always pays off in the end.

Sophia continued, "And you'll do better to earn the trust of others when you announce bad news before it hits the rumor mill, than when you're compelled to do a cleanup operation after the fact. With things like this, there will always be pain. There's no way of escaping it. But at least when you communicate proactively, you have more control over when and how you take the pain, and you will walk away with more dignity and credibility."

"But there are times I know about something early on, but just can't announce it to the workers because doing so could harm the company."

"Agreed. But this wasn't one of those times. Most workers understand there are *some* things management can't share with them. And they'll respect you for that. But as a general rule, we all hate to be kept in the dark."

> # When you leave others feeling uninformed, they will also feel devalued, and become resentful.

"So, what do you think you communicated to the workers by not communicating with them?" Sophia asked.

"I don't understand what you mean. I didn't communicate *any-thing*. That was the problem. I avoided it and left it up to Rick. And even then, the employees didn't hear about it until the cedar chips had already been removed."

"And you don't think that communicated anything to them?"

"I see your point. No wonder they're angry and scared. They must have taken my actions to mean they're not important to me…that I regard them as somehow 'lower' than myself. Like I didn't have the common decency or courage to talk about what was going on. Or maybe they think I am a phony…some kind of snake (not that I'm prejudiced against snakes or anything, but small rodents in particular are not fond of them), who just pretends to care about them as long as it's useful, but then stabs them in the back. I guess I shouldn't be surprised they suspect I'm plotting some kind of massive layoff. All I'm *really* trying to do is keep the Therapetz division lean enough to weather this storm without incurring too much damage for the company or the employees."

> # What's *not* communicated often sends a more powerful message than what *is* communicated.

"Maybe you're being a little hard on yourself, Jerry. It's obvious your intentions are good. I wonder if there may be some way you can convey what you *really* think and feel. Explain the basis of your decision. Just sit down and shoot straight with them. Communicating through Rick's note just left too much ambiguity...too much room for misunderstanding. When you don't give others enough background or context, they tend to invent their own. And their "manufactured reality" is usually more scary and malignant than anything a well-meaning boss like yourself would even dare to dream up. So, what do you say? Are you ready for another mulligan?"

"Let's get back to your discussion with Rick."

"Will do," said Rick.

"No, wait a minute, Rick," Jerry said. "I think this will go a lot better if I call a meeting in the morning so I can talk things over with everybody before we remove the cedar."

"Delaying by another day will have its costs."

"I know, but I have a feeling we'll end up paying a pretty big price if we don't take the time to talk with them first."

"Whatever you say. See you tomorrow."

"Sophia, any thoughts on what I should tell the workers about the meeting?"

As we already know, this is the kind of thing that can be easily misunderstood. You'd better deliver the meeting announcement yourself over the PA, or, if it's more practical to get out a memo to everyone, you might want to try that instead.

"I'll go with the PA."

Jerry's voice came across the system, "Good afternoon, everyone. As you know, the past few months have been a bit of a struggle for us, but I'm optimistic we'll weather this storm without doing anything too drastic. Nonetheless, I've been working with Rick Feasel for the past few days to see where we might be able to save some money. For anyone interested in what we have in mind, I'd like to invite you to participate in a brief informational session tomorrow morning, thirty minutes before the start of the first shift. I hope to see all of you there. Oh! You might want to pick up breakfast on the way. One thing we decided to cut for now is doughnuts at morning meetings. We'll still supply the coffee though. See you tomorrow."

That was well done, Jerry. Straightforward, and you gave them a taste of what the meeting will entail without causing undue alarm. I also like the fact you made the meeting voluntary. That communicates

*you respect their off-duty time, and since you're not requiring everyone
to be there, it lessens the chance they'll all go home wondering if they'll
have jobs tomorrow. Why don't we fast forward a little more so you can
get on with the morning meeting."*

"Take it away."

"Thank you for coming in early this morning…and for bring-
ing your own breakfasts. I'm glad to see such a good turnout. That
tells me how invested you are in the work you do for SCRAPPI.
Anyway, I realize many of you had to make special arrangements
to be here at this hour, and I want you to know I appreciate it.

"Well, as I began saying yesterday, the company is going
through some tough times now. There have been layoffs in other
divisions, but I think we're in good enough shape to avoid that
here for now, and hopefully, for the future. But we are going to
have to make *some* cuts. That means we'll all have to give up some
things we've become accustomed to.

"One of the more notable changes has to do with the cedar
chips in the restrooms. I know that's been a real plus to many of
you, but we stand to realize substantial savings by discontinuing
the cedar chips, and by minimizing the associated janitorial and
insurance costs."

"Why are you picking on the small rodents?" said Shirley the
mouse. "We're the ones who will suffer most from this change."

"I can see why it might look that way to you, Shirley," said Jerry.
"I suppose like most things in life, it's not entirely fair. But with
what we stand to save on expenses associated with the cedar chips,
we can continue to pay the salaries of one and a half line workers.
It seems best to sacrifice the luxury of the cedar chips in the interest of keeping a couple of good employees. Wouldn't you agree?"

"Hmm. I guess if you put it that way, it makes sense. Will we ever get the chips back?" asked Shirley.

"Well, not those *exact* chips. If we do bring them back, we'll be sure to get *new* ones." Jerry paused as the employees chuckled. "Look, I won't promise we'll bring the chips back any time soon, but I realize how important this is to many of you, and I do promise to re-examine the issue once things stabilize."

"Once more, you're doing well, Jerry. You've acknowledged Shirley's feelings about unfairness, yet avoided making empty promises. You also disarmed them a little with that crack about the used chips. I'm sure you can manage the rest of this meeting without me. It seems you've learned an important lesson today:

> # Unclear messages lead to misunderstandings, which lead to relational problems, which lead to business problems.

"Keep up the good work, and shoot me an e-mail every once in a while to let me know how things are going. Take care."

"Good-bye, Sophia. Thanks again for your help."

Mulligan's Mull-Agains

1. Am I letting anticipated pain prevent me from communicating a necessary message?

2. What price might I pay in the long term if I fail to communicate clearly now?

3. What am I communicating by my silence? What might others assume if I don't say anything?

4. What context can I provide to help others understand and accept my decisions and actions?

5. Am I falling into the trap of promising or hinting things that I'm unlikely to deliver…just to appease others?

6. Do cedar chips actually absorb odors, or merely cover them up?

7

The Shocking Truth…Revealed!

The economic crisis came and went. The Therapetz Division managed to get through it without any layoffs, though there had been additional, more painful cost-cutting measures to contend with…like removing the bubbling faux treasure chest from the goldfish lounge, and replacing the Ritz crackers in the parakeet break room with generic soda crackers. Jerry used what he'd learned from the cedar chips incident to manage these other situations effectively the *first* time around.

But that was all behind SCRAPPI now, and with sales back on track, Jerry could devote his attention to other things. By this point, he was earning a reputation throughout the company for his competence and genuine concern for the well-being of the employees.

Jerry's latest pet project was both innovative and high-tech. Borrowing from behavior therapy, his team developed a relaxation tape—the kind with ocean and forest sounds playing in the background while a soothing voice talks you through a progressive muscle relaxation sequence. The Therapetz version, however, was enhanced with virtual reality technology. Jerry called it, "Almost Paradise." The prototype would be designed for dogs, but Jerry planned to develop different versions for other species.

The subject for clinical trials was a zippy little dog named Felicia Unger. Characteristically uptight and anxious, she was the perfect one to test the efficacy of this new product. If "Almost Paradise" could calm her, it would work on anybody.

With a little help on the experimental design from Dr. Goodfur the hare and her assistant, Pavlov, Jerry decided to oversee the research himself. He was so excited about the potential of this product he wanted real hands-on involvement. A schedule was developed where Felicia was to experience the relaxation sequence twice daily at first, but then less and less frequently as she'd gain mastery over her anxiety. Each time she'd visit "Almost Paradise," Felicia was to be hooked up to a monitoring device that records muscle tension, pulse, respiration, and skin temperature so her progress could be measured. Dr. Goodfur advised Jerry to be present during the first few trials to ensure Felicia was following instructions and to troubleshoot any problems. Jerry and Felicia agreed this would be best. Upon completion of the clinical trials, Jerry would present the results to SCRAPPI's Board of Directors.

"Felicia," Jerry began, "I'd like you to start this tomorrow. I'll try to be there, but if I can't, I'll stop by later in the morning to see how things went. You will need to self-record the data from the monitoring device, but I'll visit you every couple of days so we can review your progress and adjust the schedule if necessary."

The plan sounded good to Felicia, who was eager to become a more laid-back dog, so she took the equipment home and set everything up in anticipation of her anxiety-free future.

Well, you know what they say about the best laid plans of mice, men, and dogs. Felicia did her part. She was ready to go at 7:30 a.m. Jerry couldn't make it. He'd forgotten it was his morning to drive the children to obedience school. Felicia would have to begin without him.

She got herself situated in the Lazy Pup recliner, attached the sensors to her skin, put on the virtual reality head set, and pressed "start." The beginning was very pleasant. Woodland noises—birds singing, cicadas chirping, and the sound of a cool breeze blowing through the trees at the forest's edge. In front of her, Felicia could see where the grassy meadow met the trees—pine, oak, and elm. Felicia felt herself relaxing, and the monitoring equipment confirmed this experience quantitatively.

Next came a deep and soothing voice.

"It's a comfortable summer day. The sun is shining. The scent of honeysuckle is in the air, and a gentle breeze is massaging your fur." Though she wasn't certain, Felicia could have sworn the voice belonged to none other than James Earl Bones, the famous canine actor who'd done the voice-overs for Bark Vader, and had narrated all those "feel good" phone company commercials. This felt ni-i-i-i-ice. It was *really* doing the trick.

The voice continued, "Your tail is wagging slowly and effortlessly as you lie partially covered by the shade of a large sugar maple. Feel the relaxation flow through your body. From the tips of your rear paws up through your knees and hindquarters…to your back…stomach…neck…and snout. Your whole body…loose, comfortable, and relaxed."

Felicia could literally feel the tension flowing out of her. She couldn't recall the last time she felt so peaceful, so serene. The voice went on, "Now as you turn to look back at your owner's beige house…"

Your owner's beige house??!!! Felicia was suddenly bombarded with a rush of adrenaline. She sat bolt upright and immediately shifted into fight-or-flight mode. The monitoring device began to sing with electronic alarms. Her anxiety was off the scales!

Unbeknownst to Jerry, Felicia was a longtime sufferer of pet-straumatic stress disorder, commonly known as PTSD. Years ago, she had lived with a family of humans in their beige house. It was a nice life. Felicia had full run of the property, which was bounded by one of those buried-wire mechanisms that sent a signal to a special collar to deliver a shock if its wearer ventured too close to the perimeter. Felicia endured a few jolts during the training period, but once she figured she'd be fine as long as she stayed away from the edge, there was no need to fear…or so she thought.

One summer day, Felicia's owners left her alone in the yard while they went to visit relatives. Shortly after they left, the collar suddenly malfunctioned. Throughout that day, no matter where she was in the yard, Felicia's collar delivered painful shocks randomly, and without warning. It was the most terrible of memories, and it all came rushing back upon her with "Almost Paradise."

Felicia was a mess…trembling, hyperventilating, and whimpering like a two-year-old pup on the way to the vet. There was no way she could go on with the protocol. She would never survive it. But what could she tell Jerry? This project was so important to him. How could she let him down like this? Having always struggled with assertiveness, she would wait until Jerry came over later that day. He'd see the data recordings, the claw marks on the armrests of the recliner, the wads of fur dangling from the electrodes that had been so hastily removed, and the half-empty bottle of Jack Spaniels on the coffee table. Then he'd understand how difficult this was for her, and he'd insist on finding someone else.

But Jerry never came. Instead, he telephoned around four o'clock.

"Hey Felicia, it's Jerry. Sorry I couldn't make it this morning. Forgot it was my turn for the carpool. Look, I'm in a bit of a hurry. I just wanted to check in and make sure everything is on track. I assume you had a chance to run the relaxation sequence this morning."

"Well, yeah."

"It's scary how realistic they can make that stuff these days, isn't it?"

"I'll say," Felicia replied. "It felt like the real thing."

"Data recorder work okay?"

"Uh-huh."

"That's great." Jerry continued, "Well, be sure to follow the protocol as we had it laid out. The instructions should be clear. I'll try to stop by later. Thanks. See ya."

Jerry hung up before Felicia could reply. She wondered what "later" meant. Later today? Later this week? Later when the cows come home? She left the room in hopes Jerry would be by some time soon.

About two weeks later, she received a rubber bouquet of roses from Jerry in the mail. It was the kind that squeaks when you chew on it. There was a note with the bouquet that read, "Thanks so much for taking on this project. I can't wait to see the data. I'm confident "Almost Paradise" will be a big success for Therapetz. I'll stop by soon to see how things are going. Warm regards, Jerry."

"Uh-oh," thought Felicia. "I was hoping he would stop by earlier so he could see how difficult this has been for me. Jerry will be really mad if he figures out I haven't gathered any data. What am I going to do?"

Felicia got an idea.

"Wait a minute. They've been using relaxation training with humans for decades. Jerry seemed confident this would work, and I was feeling pretty good until the beige house part. There's really no question whether this is do-able. It's just a matter of finding the right data to support what we already know. The monitors were on at my best point and at my worst. Maybe I can work within those two extremes to come up with the kind of data Jerry is looking for."

Inside, Felicia knew her thoughts were wrong, but by now she had painted herself into a corner, and this seemed to be the easiest way out.

"Surely," she thought, "Jerry's collecting data on others too. It'll all average out. Anyway, Jerry hasn't stopped by yet. If I don't draw attention to myself, he probably never will. I'll just get him the data he's looking for, and this will all be over soon."

She continued the charade, and after four more weeks, sent Jerry the data she had concocted.

Jerry was excited. According to the pilot data from Felicia, "Almost Paradise" was even more effective than he expected. Of course, he'd have to put a research team together to conduct further clinical trials before taking this new product to the market, but at least he had enough to present his idea to the Board of Directors. Jerry hoped they'd free up some additional funding for further research and production. Jerry knew this would be a shining moment in his career. He even mailed Sophia an invitation to the presentation so his mentor could share the pride of the moment. He also invited Felicia to join him in "a brief presentation and celebration of the world's newest innovation in anxiety management."

"That doesn't sound too threatening," thought Felicia. "I'd rather not go, but I guess I really ought to try and make it."

Jerry prepared well for the meeting. Mitch Shellhouser was there, as well as Rae Zorr and the board members. A few others attended, including representatives from R&D, Sales, Production, and of course, Felicia. Jerry made sure there was an extra chair for Sophia, even though no one else would be aware of her presence.

The moment of truth had arrived. The presentation started off well enough. Jerry provided a brief description of the product and its intended use, then began to describe the results of the pilot he had conducted with Felicia.

Some of the board members were a bit skeptical—particularly Dr. Gallop, a quarter horse who distinguished himself as a researcher in animal behavior. Unfortunately, Jerry was not as familiar with the pilot as he needed to be in order to intelligently respond to Dr. Gallop's questions.

"Mr. Mulligan," Gallop said, "It's quite unusual to see such a steady linear progression uniformly across all measures. You'll most typically see slow initial gains until the subject achieves some degree of mastery, then more progress by about the second week. And finally, a leveling off as the subject approaches their maximal benefit from the training. Are you confident of the integrity of your data?"

"Uh, that's a good point, Dr. Gallop," Jerry replied nervously, as he glanced at Felicia. "I, too, was a bit surprised by the pattern of results. Um, but, uh...." Then Jerry did something uncharacteristic. Trying to salvage what was becoming a bad situation, he pulled an explanation out of thin air. "...the data you refer to were generally gathered under laboratory conditions, while our pilot, though less methodologically rigorous, was conducted in the subject's natural environment. My behavioral observations of Ms. Unger during the experiment were consistent with the linear progression seen in the biological measures."

"Jerry, what are you doing?" asked Sophia.

"Cut to the chase, Jerry," interrupted Rae. "What are you trying to say?"

"I'm saying that the data are sound."

"Careful, Jerry."

Still skeptical, Gallop proposed, "This 'Almost Paradise' relaxation protocol sounds pretty good. I'd like to see it work." Then, turning to Felicia, Gallop said, "Perhaps you would be kind enough to give us a demonstration."

A look of panic crossed Felicia's face. How would she get out of this one?

"I can't do that, Dr. Gallop."

"Why not?"

Then, turning to Jerry, Felicia said, "I'm sorry I let you down, Jerry, but Dr. Gallop is right. I never once got through the entire sequence. I couldn't do it, so I fabricated the data."

Realizing there was no way out at this point, Jerry cried, "Sophia, help me out here!"

"Jerry, what's going on!?"

"That's what *I'm* wondering! I can't believe what Felicia just did! She must have been lying to me all along. What would possess her to do something like that? Dogs are supposed to be loyal and true! She totally betrayed me. That lazy, manipulative hound. How could she sit there in front of all those animals and act like the experiment was some great success? Would it have been so hard to tell me she didn't have the data? If there's one thing I can't stand, it's dishonesty!"

There was silence for a few seconds. Sophia responded, almost monotone, "Are you finished?"

"*I'm* not, but I wish I could say the same for my career! Can I have my mulligan now? I want to go back a few weeks, march right up to Felicia's house, and catch her in the act of falsifying that data. And when I do, I'm going to chew her out like an old leather boot!"

"You're not ready for your mulligan yet. First, I want you to consider what you just said."

"Which part?"

"For starters, the part about how much you can't stand dishonesty."

"Yeah?"

"I'm wondering, would the lie you just told to Dr. Gallop and the board fall under your definition of 'dishonesty'?"

Jerry softened. He knew Sophia was right. There was no excuse for his behavior. It would have been far better to answer Gallop's first question truthfully. Yes, it would have made him look bad to admit he had not supervised the experiment properly, or he could not ensure the integrity of the data. But not as bad as he looked after getting caught in a lie. He just learned a very important lesson:

> # The admission of ignorance or failure is less destructive than an exposed cover-up. Tell it like it is.

"Why did you lie, Jerry?"
Jerry paused a moment.
"I don't know. I was feeling on the spot and then things started unraveling so quickly. I just didn't want to look like an idiot up there. Stretching the truth seemed like the only way out. I figured I could skate by with a white lie and straighten things out afterward. But then I kept digging my hole deeper."

> # Confess your mistakes while they're still small.

"Yeah, I'd say you dug deep pretty fast. I wonder if maybe Felicia lied for similar reasons. Not that that would excuse her behavior, but maybe her intent was not as malicious as you're assuming."
Jerry smiled sheepishly as he shook his head.
"What are you thinking?" Sophia asked.
"I'm really embarrassed. I shouldn't have to be told these things. Am I the dumbest guy you've ever fairy-godmothered, or what?"
"Not by a long shot. I've been at this a long time, Jerry, and have coached some very accomplished pets and people. Most make the same

kinds of mistakes you do, and could stand to sharpen their communication and relational skills. Some, often those in the highest positions, think they've got it all sewn up, and believe this kind of help is only for those who are new to management. But almost always, a brief discussion with their subordinates or peers reveals these leaders over-estimate themselves. They miss the opportunity to improve because they lack insight, don't solicit anyone else's assessment of their behavior, or haven't fostered enough trust with their associates for anyone to give them honest feedback. The ones who grow the most are those, like you, who see their shortcomings, embrace critical feedback, and constantly strive to improve."

"That makes me feel a little better."

"It should. Anyway, Jerry, back to your situation. You talked about your own behavioral observations of Felicia during the experiment. It's obvious now you never actually observed her. Why didn't you?"

"I intended to. In fact, I told her a few times I'd be over to see her. Other things got in the way, and I never got around to it. The few times I called, it seemed like everything was going according to plan, so it didn't seem important that I stop by."

"What did you teach Felicia about yourself by failing to do what you said you would do?"

"I never figured I was *teaching* her anything, but I can see maybe I was. I guess I gave her the message that I don't really mean what I say."

"That's right, Jerry. And when you don't actually do what you say you will do, you train others to ignore what comes out of your mouth. Your words, in effect, lose their meaning and their power."

> # When you break promises, you train others to ignore your words.

"So by telling Felicia I was coming by to check on things, but then never doing so, I trained her to expect no accountability to me for her work."

"*Correct.*"

"In time, it must have become harder and harder for her to tell me the truth even if she wanted to. Maybe she found herself digging a hole with respect to me, just as I did with respect to the board."

> # If you want others to communicate with candor, make it easy for them to do so.

"Now, Jerry, I think you're ready for your mulligan."

The clock returned to the first day of the experiment, to Jerry's afternoon phone call to Felicia. He already committed to stop by her house that day.

"Hey, Felicia, it's Jerry. Sorry I couldn't make it this morning. Forgot it was my turn for the carpool. It's been a crazy day. I promise I'll stop by in about two hours, on my way home from the office. We can talk more then, but for now, I just wanted to check in and make sure everything is on track. I assume you had a chance to run the relaxation sequence this morning."

"Well, yeah."

"It's scary how realistic they can make that stuff these days, isn't it?"

"I'll say," Felicia replied. "It felt like the real thing."

"Data recorder work okay?"

"Uh-huh."

"That's great." Jerry continued, "I'll see you about six o'clock. Thanks. See ya."

As he hung up the phone, Jerry said to Sophia, "That happened just about the same way I remembered it. Felicia gave no indication that anything was wrong."

"You're right; she didn't. But you know, you never really asked her how it went. You told her what you assumed, and you asked her if the recorder worked, but you could have learned a lot more from this conversation had you asked better, more open-ended questions. Too often, managers ask vague questions like, 'Is everything okay?' or 'Do you understand?' and then they're shocked when they later find out some things weren't okay; or important details were not understood. Most of us tend to answer such general questions affirmatively even when we shouldn't. Doing so allows us to hide our insecurity or incompetence, and it saves us the effort of having to articulate lengthy explanations. Sometimes, we answer that way simply because we don't want to burden others with our own problems."

"Kind of like when others ask me 'How's it going?' I almost always answer, 'Pretty good,' even when I'm miserable."

"That's right. When it's critical to have a clear understanding of what's going on, push a little harder for specific information. So, instead of asking, 'Do you understand?' say something like, 'I know I've just given you a lot of information. So I can be sure I conveyed my expectations clearly, tell me your understanding of what I've asked you to do.' Or, you could ask something as simple as, 'So, what do you think you'll do?' or, 'How are you planning to handle it?' Now the respondent must demonstrate understanding rather than just claim to have understood. Likewise, instead of asking, 'Is everything okay?' you might want to say something like, 'How about giving me the run-down on what you accomplished with the project today.'"

> # When it's important to stay on top of a situation, ask questions that require specific answers.

Jerry kept his word and stopped to see Felicia on his way home. A quick glance around her apartment provided ample evidence of how poorly "Almost Paradise" had gone for her. Jerry asked some specific questions to ascertain how he could help Felicia. While he still felt disappointed she did not come clean with him the first time around, his anger diminished, as he could now appreciate how difficult this whole incident had been for her.

As is usually the case for someone who is granted limitless mulligans, Jerry managed to turn the situation around and get "Almost Paradise" and his career back on track. He found other subjects for the pilot study, which he turned over to professional researchers (though he did keep a close eye on the status of the project). Most importantly, he encouraged Felicia to seek treatment for her PTSD. She found a capable psychologist and, as a testimony to the hard work she put into her therapy, Felicia eventually managed to get through "Almost Paradise" with only minimal anxiety. In a sense, she too, had been granted a mulligan, and this time, she finished the course.

Mulligan's Mull-Agains

1. Is there sufficient alignment between my words and my actions that others can trust that I mean what I say?

2. Am I consistently honest in my reporting practices, even when doing so might reflect negatively on my own performance?

3. What can I do to foster conditions in which others can feel free to tell me the truth, even when I might not like what they have to say?

4. How can I more accurately assess my own communication effectiveness? Who, besides myself, can I go to for insight in this area? What can I do to make it easier for others to give me candid feedback?

5. Am I accepting generalized answers that merely confirm what I hope to hear, or do I need to dig deeper to get more detailed information?

6. Do random zappings in the workplace leave *people* feeling anxious too?

8

Trophy Cat or Catastrophe?

D. Claude Shirker was a domestic short-haired cat who had been with the company for almost twenty-five years. Like Bud Green the iguana, Claude (as he preferred to be called) was a production supervisor. In fact, the two had served in the military together, and remained close throughout the years.

Claude was talented, and in his earlier days, quite driven. At one point, he was being groomed for a top management position, but never made it. Years ago, this once rising star saw his career plummet faster than a yo-yo with a broken string. Perhaps he resented having been passed over too many times for the Employee of the Year award. Maybe he just lost confidence after his wife ran off with the milkman. Or, quite possibly, his years of hard drinking had finally taken their toll (unlike Felicia, Claude preferred Catty Sark). Whatever the reasons, this former feline marvel had become a lazy and irresponsible slug, (figuratively speaking; no disrespect to slugs intended). At this point, he was doing little more than marking time until retirement.

Since the introduction of the Therapetz line, Claude had supervised first shift production for Summer Bright ultra bright lighting units, which were used for treatment of seasonal affective disorder (SAD) in pets. Like people, many pets experience this severe form of the winter blues. All those cold, gray short days living cooped up in the house can drive pets to despair. By exposing these animals to prolonged periods of intense light—much like exposure to real sunshine—their depression can improve enough to get them through until spring. No doubt about it, the Summer Bright line was hot!

This particular year, after a famous celebrity publicly announced that light therapy had helped her overcome SAD, demand for Summer Bright lights had been outpacing production capacity. If there was ever a time Jerry Mulligan needed Claude to deliver, this was it. But Claude was the kind who, if feeling pushed, would be sure to push back even harder…and Jerry knew it. In fact, Jerry was intimidated by Claude. He felt it was generally better to ignore Claude than to challenge him.

The tension grew. Despite the fact a large number of employees under his supervision were working overtime, Claude showed no willingness to go the extra mile himself. He routinely arrived at work late and missed important meetings, yet dealt harshly with those he supervised. He'd been caught catnapping on three separate occasions. On this particular day, Claude made a rather large mistake…something that could not be ignored.

He had assigned the task of final inspection of Summer Bright lights to three mice named Ratón, Souris, and Topo. Truth be known, Claude never much liked mice, except between two slices of whole wheat bread with Dijon mustard and a splash of Tabasco sauce. But he was never known to treat them unfairly.

Anyway, the process required inspectors to examine carefully each Summer Bright light before it left the plant floor. To do this, the inspectors had to turn the lights on and look directly into the units to ensure each photocell was functioning properly. Normally, inspectors would wear special sunglasses to protect their eyes. But because the standard-issue sunglasses were designed for underwater sea monkeys, they simply would not fit the mice's heads, and therefore could not be worn. Needless to say, this took a serious toll on the mice's vision. They had become, quite literally (albeit temporarily), three blind mice.

An honest mistake? Probably. But in today's litigious society, there's a price tag on every error, and a throng of lawyers out to stick somebody with the tab. Naturally, the Risk Management (RM) and Humane Resources (HR) departments were in a dither about this one. Fortunately, Ratón, Souris, and Topo were not the vindictive types. And once their vision returned, they figured, "At least we didn't lose our tails or anything." So, to everyone's relief (except their lawyers), they opted not to sue. But Claude's error had been harmful and costly, and had to be addressed.

Jerry did not want to deal with this one. He knew he should have confronted Claude's attitude and irresponsible behavior long ago, but avoidance was the path of least resistance. With the RM and HR departments pressuring him to take action, the time for confrontation had arrived.

As Jerry paced his office floor searching for the best way to approach Claude, Bud Green stopped by to drop off some paperwork.

"Bud," Jerry began, "You seem to know Claude pretty well."

"That's right, we served in the military together. We've been friends for years. What's the matter? Is that old cat dragging his feet too much again?"

"Well, there's more to it." Jerry continued to explain the background of the situation to Bud, ending with, "So I've got to say *something* to the guy, but I don't know what."

Then Jerry got an idea.

"I wonder, Bud, if it might be better for *you* to talk about this with Claude. He might be able to hear things better coming from an old friend than from me."

"I guess so, but what do you want me to say?"

"We can discuss that later. What do you say? Are you willing to do it?"

Bud mumbled, "Do I really have a choice?"

So, Jerry instructed Bud to confront his long-time peer concerning the feline's tardiness, laziness, and especially his gross inattention to procedural details in the three-mouse situation. Bud would reluctantly carry out the dirty work.

The next day arrived. Bud tossed and turned the night before, worrying and rehearsing how he might approach Claude. He knew Claude could be a little touchy, and he didn't handle criticism well. Yet Bud did not want to jeopardize the friendship. The more he thought about it, the more he came to resent Jerry for putting this difficult task on his shoulders.

Well, an iguana's gotta do what an iguana's gotta do. So Bud arranged to meet Claude for lunch. He chose Claude's favorite eatery, "Bobcat Evans." Claude arrived late, of course.

It had been a few months since they had gotten together. So the two critters made the usual small talk, relived a few memories from their days in the service, and expressed their mutual longing for times when life was a lot simpler at SCRAPPI.

Claude could sense Bud's growing discomfort.

"You're not yourself, Bud. You've taken only two bites of your cricket burger and you've barely touched that pile of flies. I haven't seen you eat like this since you got that Dear John letter back in '74. When Bud Green can't eat, something's always wrong. Now come clean. What is it?"

"I didn't realize it was that obvious." Bud paused for a moment, then continued. "There is something, Claude."

"Well, spit it out!"

"Claude, this isn't easy for me. Look, Jerry Mulligan asked me to talk to you."

"*Mulligan* did? What's he got to say to me? Does this have something to do with those three mice? That was an accident, Bud. I learned my lesson. It'll never happen again."

"It's that…but there's more. Claude, they aren't too happy with your performance lately. They say you've been late a lot, you don't seem to care anymore, and you haven't been pulling your weight."

"Not pulling my weight!?" Claude was getting louder. "I've been busting my tail with this company for the past twenty-five years! I was stacking eighty-pound boxes of choke collars when Jerry Mulligan was sucking his thumb!"

"Jerry doesn't have a thumb. He's a dog."

"Yeah, whatever. You've seen what I've been through with this company, Bud. Are *you* telling me I'm lazy?"

"Easy, Claude, I'm just the messenger here. You know how it is. Those guys in the big offices don't know what it's really like in the trenches. They sit in meetings and go on those golf outings, and then tell us we don't work hard enough. I'm just looking out for you. *They're* not happy with your work, and I've been asked to talk to you about it."

Bud paused a few seconds, "Look, just be careful. That's all. They're watching now. Be on your best behavior for the next few weeks and this will all blow over."

"Yeah, I know how that game works." Claude paused, "You know, if Mulligan's got a problem with me, I wish that coward would tell me to my face. I can't believe he sent you to do this."

"I wasn't real happy about it either," replied Bud.

Bud and Claude finished their meals and headed back to the plant. Claude was angry. He felt unappreciated and mistreated. For the next several weeks, he did what was necessary to appear like a model supervisor whenever upper management was watching. But he bad-mouthed Jerry every chance he got, and did what he could to foster an "us versus them" mentality among the workers he supervised.

Bud, too, harbored some resentment. The trust and respect he had begun to develop for Jerry was eroding.

Sure, Claude got the message about his performance problems, but productivity on the line continued to suffer, and now two of Jerry's key Production Supervisors had attitude problems…definitely not the outcome Jerry had been hoping for. Jerry sensed he had mishandled this situation somehow, so he summoned Sophia with the whistle she had given him. He needed another mulligan.

Jerry told Sophia what had happened. Of course, he had no idea what transpired between Claude and Bud at lunch that day. Even Flora couldn't help him on that one, as her friend Ucho the fly rarely ventured outside the walls of the plant. Sophia, however, had seen enough of these kinds of situations to put the pieces together.

"Jerry, why did you send Bud to confront Claude? That was your job."

"You told me a good manager has to delegate. I was just following the advice you gave."

"Yes, Jerry, I have told you to delegate. But delegation isn't about finding someone else to do all the things you don't want to. It's about making the most of your team's talents to get the job done, and about empowering others so they can grow. In giving this task to Bud, you were merely trying to avoid something you were afraid to do yourself."

Avoiding difficult conversations rarely solves problems.

"But I was giving Bud an opportunity to learn and grow, wasn't I?"

"No, I think you did little more than misuse his prior relationship with Claude. If you were interested in Bud's professional development, you would have provided more oversight, direction, and feedback. Bud didn't gain anything from this."

"I think I see your point. To be honest, I'm not sure *I* know how to handle this one, much less teach Bud how to."

"That's one of the things I really appreciate about you, Jerry Mulligan. You're honest enough with yourself, and with me, that you can learn from your mistakes. I wish more creatures were like that."

"Thanks. It's good to see I'm doing *something* right."

"We can talk about the hazards of sending someone else to do these kinds of confrontations, and I can help you learn to manage them better yourself."

"That sounds good to me."

"First, you have to remember that, like you, others tend to avoid challenging confrontations. Bud didn't want to deal with Claude any more than you did…even if he agreed with your assessment of Claude's performance. In this case, Bud was the bearer of your message. He didn't own it himself. He knew that, and Claude probably picked up on it too. They both knew the message was yours, but you sent a proxy. What message do you think *that* sent?"

"Hmm. They probably think I'm a chicken. Well, not literally, but you know what I mean."

"Jerry, how would you feel if Mitch Shellhouser had a problem with your performance, but sent one of your peers to deal with you rather than addressing you himself?"

"I guess I'd be kind of angry. I would wonder why Mitch didn't have the decency to deal with me face-to-face. You know, I trust folks more when I know they shoot straight with me…when I know I can count on them to tell me what they don't like as well as what they do like. I respect them for it."

"Exactly. And if there are any questions or defensiveness from the one receiving the feedback, it's easier to respond clearly and constructively when the one delivering the message is also one who owns it."

Criticism is best received when delivered by someone who owns it.

"But Mitch sometimes asks me to deliver difficult messages to *my* subordinates. Isn't he guilty of the same thing?"

"While it might sometimes be best for Mitch to handle such matters himself, the two situations are really quite different. You see, as *your* supervisor, Mitch has every right to ask *you* to deal with your own direct reports. That's protocol in many organizations. But it would be pretty squirrelly, however, for Mitch to ask you to confront another one of *his* direct reports…one of your peers. That's what you did by asking Bud to deal with Claude. Besides, Mitch is responsible for his behavior, and you're responsible for yours."

Sophia continued, "Bud's not interested in making enemies with you or with Claude. You're Bud's boss. Bud wanted to please you, so he did what he was told. Claude is Bud's peer and longtime friend, and I doubt he wanted that to change. So he probably worked pretty hard to be sure Claude would still see him as a good guy. The easiest way for Bud to preserve these two valuable relationships is to say what you want to hear when he's alone with you, and say what Claude wants to hear when he's alone with Claude."

"But that's kind of two-faced."

"I suppose, but it was the easy route for Bud to take. And you didn't do much to provide him with the skills or guidance to navigate the more difficult path…one that would require him to tactfully balance his responsibilities to you and the company with his responsibilities to his peers and subordinates."

> Those placed in the middle usually lean toward whoever is closer at the moment.

"Now that you know *why* it was counterproductive to send in Bud to do your work, let's talk about how you might have been able to approach Claude yourself."

"Okay, Sophia, I'm all ears."

"First, Jerry, you need to remember when you have a trouble spot, you've got to monitor the situation closely. If you find cockroach droppings in your doghouse, you have to spray the place and then check periodically to make sure they've left and haven't come back. Likewise, with Claude's performance problems, you should have found ways to monitor his behavior on a regular basis. For example, simply tracking his sign-in sheet would have enabled you to objectively measure his punctuality."

"That makes sense. But when monitoring reveals performance problems, how do you deal with someone like Claude? I mean, the first thing I thought of was to discipline him through some form of punishment."

"Is there any sort of punishment that's proven effective for Claude?" asked Sophia.

"Well, yes, there was *one* thing…but how many times can you neuter a guy and still expect it to work?"

"Good point, Jerry. You know, punishment can be an effective teaching method, especially when you're going for impact and want the offender to rapidly learn the gravity of his or her errors. Nonetheless, we usually learn more effectively through reinforcement than through punishment. So, first you want to make sure you regularly pay attention to the good things Claude does, not just the bad. So many workers only hear from their bosses when there is a problem. If you, as a manager, only spend time with your subordinates when problems arise, you will condition them to be defensive every time you come around. In effect, if you fail to attend to the good, yet punish or criticize every time there is a problem, you train others to avoid you and defend *against* you rather than to inform you and cooperate *with* you. Surely there are some things Claude does well. Catch him doing things *right* from time to time. Then he'll be more willing to hear what you have to say when you do offer constructive criticism."

Remember to comment on the good stuff.

Sophia went on, "Be positive and constructive. Criticize the undesirable *behaviors* without being *personally* critical."

"I don't understand what you mean."

"For example, rather than characterizing Claude as 'irresponsible' or 'lazy,' it's much better to stick with observables."

"Observables?"

"Yes. Behaviors that can be observed and objectively measured. Like the percentage of days when Claude clocks in on time versus late. Or his attendance at team meetings. Or the number of injuries among the workers he supervises. By measuring such things, you can set clearer performance expectations, and minimize subjectivity about whether or not the expectations are being met. You know, it's difficult to objectively assess whether someone has become 'more responsible' or 'less lazy,' but it's easy to identify improvements in punctuality, attendance, and attention to safety. Also, when you are specific about performance issues, it is much easier to improve upon them. I wouldn't know where to start improving myself if someone told me I was irresponsible. But if they told me I was late to work thirty percent of the time, and they expected me to get to less than five percent, I'd know exactly what to do in order to satisfy them. Then it's no longer a matter of opinion. The evidence for my performance would be obvious and indisputable."

> # If you want something to improve, you must find a way to measure it.

"That makes sense," said Jerry. "Any other thoughts about how to deal with Claude?"

"Yes, there are a few other things you might want to consider. When you offer corrective feedback, be sure to put things in context...help the employee understand why it's important they change."

"What if it's not important?"

"If it's not important, you shouldn't be correcting it. You should spend your time on things that matter. So," continued Sophia, "tell me why it matters that Claude show up on time for work each day."

"There are lots of reasons," Jerry replied. "But the most important is tardiness sets a bad example for others. I mean, if the supervisor doesn't show up on time, he'll have no credibility when he demands others be punctual."

"And why does it matter that the others be punctual?"

"Duh! If the production workers don't show up on time, productivity drops, then costs rise, then prices rise, then consumers buy from the competition instead, then we have to cut jobs...*everybody* loses."

"Jerry, that's how *you* think from an executive's point of view. You can't assume everyone connects the dots the same way you do. When you address performance problems, be sure to provide context. Help others to reason through the issues so they too can appreciate the implications of their behavior. You need to help Claude see your primary concern is not that he conforms to the rules, but that the company performs well."

"I've tried to tell him that before, but it just turns into an argument every time."

"Well then don't *tell* him what you think. Instead, ask him the kinds of questions that will *lead* him to sound conclusions...questions that will help him develop the reasoning skills you'd like him to have."

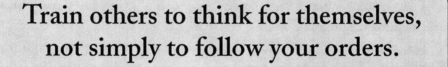

Train others to think for themselves, not simply to follow your orders.

"I think I understand," said Jerry. "How about if I try that now?"

Jerry was once again transported to the past. This time, instead of asking Bud to do his dirty work, Jerry confronted Claude himself. As Jerry expected, he found Claude in the break room, relaxing over a cat-puccino.

"Hey, Claude."

"Jerry."

"I saw your granddaughter's picture in the paper on Tuesday. Wow, valedictorian! I can't believe she's finished high school already. Last time you brought her in, she seemed so little. Time sure flies."

"Yeah, I can't believe she's eighteen already. She got herself a college scholarship. Says she wants to come back here and be my boss someday." Claude chuckled. "I guess that means she's after your job, Mulligan."

Jerry and Claude engaged in small talk for a few more minutes. Claude finished his beverage, and then said, "Well, I guess I'd better get back to work."

"See you later, Claude."

"Yeah, later Jerry."

"Jerry, why are you letting him leave? You never even mentioned the performance issues?"

"Relax, Sophia. I know what I'm doing. That was the first time I have talked with Claude about personal stuff in years. It felt like we were connecting."

"Are you sure you weren't just avoiding the confrontation again?"

"I'm sure. I didn't want Claude feeling like I was just following that old formula about complimenting someone just before you hit them with criticism. Like you said, I don't want to condition him to dread every interaction with me. I'll talk with him about the performance issues tomorrow...I promise. Besides, with your powers, we can fast forward to that moment right away, so I'm not really procrastinating any pain now, am I?"

"I guess you do know what you're doing."

Instantaneously, it became the next morning. Jerry went to Claude's office. He felt meeting on Claude's turf would be less threatening than asking Claude to report to his office.

"Hey Claude, do you have a few minutes? I need to talk with you about some things."

"What things?"

"Well," Jerry began, "I'm concerned that production has been off-pace for the month. We've got to do something to catch up with the orders, or we're going to have some angry customers on our hands."

"What do you want me to do about it?" Claude snapped. "I told you we needed to hire."

"I know. And I think that would be the route to go if Summer Bright didn't have such a pronounced seasonal sales pattern. If we hire now, when we're getting lots of orders, we won't get the new workers trained for at least another six weeks. And by that time, sales should begin to tail off. Based on this year's sales, we can anticipate the seasonal increase next year, and can consider hiring temp workers in the early fall, *before* demand increases. I'm not sure we have any other options aside from overtime at this point."

"I'm pushing the guys as hard as I know how," Claude replied. "Some of them just don't want the hours."

"Look, Claude. You know how critical it is for us to get the product out on time. What can you do to help your team understand this? How can you *demonstrate* your commitment to the productivity goals that you're asking them to achieve?"

"Good, Jerry, you're training him to think like a problem-solver."

"I don't know, Mulligan. What are you driving at?"

"Nice try, Jerry, but he's not going to make this easy on you."

"Claude, I apologize for not having this discussion with you sooner. I knew productivity was down, and should have talked with you when I first noticed we had a problem."

"Keep going Jerry. Smart move offering the apology for your role in the problem. That should make him less defensive when you address his role."

Jerry continued, "I wonder if you might not get others on board for overtime if you put in extra hours yourself for the next few weeks."

"Are you calling me lazy?"

"Nope. Hand me the labor reports, though, and we can see if and where we might be able to increase your hours." Jerry took a few moments to review the reports.

"Claude, you've come in late three out of the last five days, and have not worked more than thirty-nine hours during any of the last six weeks. You're going to have a hard time recruiting anyone to work overtime unless you show you're willing to go the extra mile yourself."

"Way to quantify and keep things objective. You are doing an excellent job modulating the emotional intensity of this exchange."

> # When things get tense, restrain your emotional expressiveness, and temper your words. Be direct, but neutral.

"Jerry, I have put in years of extra miles. How dare you suggest I'm not pulling my weight around here?!"

"Claude, you've worked here a long time, and you've brought a great deal to the company. But if you slack off now, it will hurt the company and your leadership credibility. You have a choice. If you want reduced hours, I'll try to arrange that. But I'm not going to allow that in your current position. If you want to remain a supervisor, you'll have to meet the expectations of a leader. And that means, among other things, you need to be on time each day, and show a willingness to work extra hours when necessary. Again, it's your choice. You tell me what you want. Once you've made your choice, let's review our mutual expectations. Either way, I'll expect you to act in accordance with the choice you've made. Will two days be long enough for you to make your decision?"

"I didn't know you could be so firm, Jerry. You tried the gentle route first, but when Claude became difficult, you calmly stood your ground. I also like the fact you gave Claude a choice. You used the word 'choice' four times. In doing so, you reinforced a critical message, placing responsibility for Claude's behavior right where it belongs...on Claude."

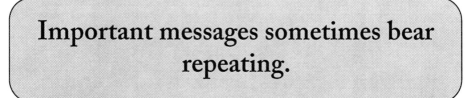

Important messages sometimes bear repeating.

Important messages sometimes bear repeating.

"You also set the stage for a subsequent discussion in which you can review performance expectations, regardless of which choice Claude makes, and set up a system for continuous monitoring. You can't sacrifice an organization's health in favor of a sick individual. If you do, you communicate to the rest of the organization that personalities, rather than mission, vision, values and goals, drive the company."

"Thanks, Sophia. As always, you've been a big help. I know where to take this one from here."

Mulligan's Mull-Agains

1. Am I shirking responsibility by sending someone else to deliver a message that I must rightfully own?

2. Am I delegating in the interest of teaching and empowering others, or simply to avoid something I find distasteful?

3. Am I communicating enough about the good things I see, or do others generally only hear from me when there is a problem?

4. How can I better use measuring and monitoring to communicate expectations, and to keep myself informed of what's going on around me?

5. As I communicate direction, am I taking the time to teach others to think for themselves?

6. Do the depression-reducing effects of ultra-bright lighting wear off when the electric bill arrives?

9

Last, But not Leashed

Jerry was jolted awake at 4:30 a.m. by the sound of his alarm clock. He took a few seconds to shake off his pre-dawn grogginess before remembering he had an early flight to Chicago for a convention. Jerry showered and dressed, and then wolfed down two bowls of Lucky Charms, which, to his surprise, he found magically delicious even at such an early hour. He peeked in on each of the children, then gave his wife Gertrude, who was still fast asleep, a gentle lick on the cheek before leaving for the airport.

Jerry's flight was uneventful, despite that FAA regulations required him to travel in the cargo hold amidst the luggage and common household pets. He found this degrading, but as a top executive at SCRAPPI, at least Jerry had a comfortable top-of-the-line pet carrier for the trip. His was upholstered with genuine leather and equipped with climate control, a sound system, a refrigerator, and a power outlet for his laptop computer.

Upon arrival, Jerry caught a limousine to his hotel, unpacked his things, and headed downstairs to the convention hall. It was time to register for the 23rd Annual Meeting of the North American Psychological Society (aka "NAPS").

As an Irish setter and non-psychologist, Jerry felt out of his element. Nonetheless, as Director of Operations for Therapetz, the convention afforded him the opportunity to establish some important contacts and generate ideas for new Therapetz products. As he skimmed through the convention program, Jerry saw there were presentations on things like "Pavlovian Conditioning" and "Learned Helplessness." He wondered if that sort of research could possibly generalize beyond humans, to other animal species.

"This is going to be boring," he thought to himself. "No wonder they call this organization 'NAPS.' I'll certainly be taking a few of them as I sit through these sessions!"

It was only one day into the convention and Jerry was already feeling cooped up. So he decided to get away from the hotel for a few hours and walk the downtown area. It seemed like a good idea, but this wasn't Carson Ridge—people treated animals differently here. What Jerry didn't realize was Chicago had a special ordinance that required all dogs, corporate executives or not, to be tethered to human beings. That's right—Jerry Mulligan violated the city's leash law. Three blocks from the hotel, he was quickly nabbed by one of Chicago's finest, Officer Willie Ketchum[1]. Jerry was cuffed, read his Miranda rights, and carted off to the police station in the caged back seat of a squad car. How humiliating!

Within hours, Jerry was brought before the magistrate, a Ms. Helena Gavel. Jerry plead guilty, was fined one hundred dollars, and sentenced to ten hours of community service. Jerry told Ms. Gavel he was in town on business, and expected to leave within a couple of days. He urged her to consider dropping the community service, as it would be difficult for him to travel back to Chicago to complete it. Ms. Gavel asked a few questions, and upon learning Jerry was an executive for a large corporation, reduced his sentence to two hours of community service. As luck would have it, the honorable magistrate's teenage daughter was the President of the

---

1. The story you are about to read is true (well, at least as true as the other stories in this book); however, the names were changed to protect the innocent.

local Junior Business Achiever's club, and the speaker they had booked for the following evening canceled on short notice. If Jerry would agree to fill in, Ms. Gavel would waive the remaining eight hours of community service. It was a deal.

Jerry took a cab back to the hotel. Once in the privacy of his room, he summoned Sophia.

"Thank goodness you came!" Jerry exclaimed. "You've got to rewind this one! I have this terrible stain on my record, and now I have to give a talk to a bunch of human teenagers. If you can just rewind it to the moment I left the hotel, then I can go right back inside and erase this whole mess!"

"I don't know, Jerry."

"What do you mean you don't know? Get me out of this!"

"Jerry," Sophia said, "I have been giving you mulligans to help you *learn*, not to keep you out of trouble. I know you don't really deserve to have a criminal record just for venturing out of your hotel. But I wonder if speaking to the Junior Business Achievers might prove to be a great learning opportunity—for you and the students."

"Whaaat!!?" Jerry replied. "What would a pack of entrepreneurial teenage humans want to hear from a dog like me?"

"Why don't you teach them about workplace communication? You've become very good at it. If they are in Junior Business Achievers because they someday want to succeed in business, then you have something valuable to give them."

"You're not going to let me off the hook, are you?"

"Nope."

"Then I guess I'd better get to work on this presentation. Will you be there in case I need you?"

"As always," Sophia replied. "I know you've got work to do, so I'll leave you to it. See you tomorrow."

"Good night, Sophia."

Jerry spent that evening and the next day preparing for his presentation. During the past few years, he had become comfortable with public speaking, an essential skill for anyone in a leadership position. But he found himself uncharacteristically nervous this time. He was used to addressing house pets and business people, but would he be able to connect with human teenagers?

Jerry knew it was important to be genuine and natural, and to find some personal common ground between himself and his audience—this would earn him greater credibility and help him engage the teens more effectively. But Jerry wasn't one to keep up on music, television, video games or fashion. Attempting to fake it, he thought, would most certainly backfire. So, he opted instead to open with a funny story about his eleventh grade literature class, in which all of his fellow students were dogs. Jerry's teacher had a peculiar style of speaking, and had an especially difficult time pronouncing the term "heartwarming classic." Instead, it usually came out sounding more like, "Heartworm in class...Ick!" which would be like saying to a group of humans, "There's a rat on the floor...Yikes!" Jerry thought this would be an effective lead-in to the topic of communication.

Jerry caught a cab to the school where the Junior Business Achievers were meeting. He had arrived early so he could shake everyone's hand as they entered the room. The students seemed impressed by this, but a couple of the smart alecks came around several times to see if Jerry could also sit, lie down, and roll over. Jerry felt insulted, and was incredulous at their lack of cultural sensitivity, but he politely ignored their commands and controlled his anger. There were a few adults in the room, one sitting next to Jerry.

When it was time to commence the meeting, another one of the adults stood up in front to introduce the evening's speaker.

"In the world of business, you've got to be able to communicate effectively to get things done. As you will see, tonight's speaker works in the kind of setting where the potential for miscommunication is high, and its consequences can be severe."

As he gestured toward the man sitting next to Jerry, the announcer continued, "So please join me in offering a warm welcome to Mr. Jerry Mulligan, who apparently has brought his dog along, as he speaks with us about the pet therapy services his company provides."

That was the last straw! Did these nincompoops think Jerry was some dog trainer's stooge whose raison d'être was merely to entertain and comfort lonely humans!? Jerry had endured enough humiliation in this town already. He summoned Sophia, who promptly appeared.

"Sophia, this doesn't look like it's turning out to be the wonderful learning experience you planned for me. Can't you PLEASE get me out of this NOW!?"

"Take it easy, Jerry. These people aren't from Carson Ridge. They're not used to dogs who behave like you. They're just assuming you're like the dogs they know. If you stick with this, maybe you'll get a chance to broaden their horizons. Let's do it again. And this time, when you first meet these people, TALK to them as you offer your paw. Tell them who you are and what you do."

"All right, I'll give it another try."

Jerry started again, carefully following Sophia's instructions. Though he still had to endure a few smart remarks, most of the students reacted to him more favorably. And because Jerry actively sought out the adult who was in charge, he was able to assure he received a proper introduction.

Jerry's opening story went well. The Junior Business Achievers were beginning to warm up to him quickly.

Jerry went on to describe a model of communication that could serve as a guide in just about any workplace situation. It was useful for personal situations, too. He explained how nearly everything he knew about workplace communication could be understood within this framework. As Jerry spoke, he sketched the model on a flip chart and called it "Mulligan's Model for Communication Effectiveness" (see appendix).

Jerry asked the students, "Why do you think it is so important for people who work together to communicate effectively?"

There were a few moments of silence. Then Ms. Gavel's daughter, Wanda, spoke up.

"Well," she postulated, "I guess in any organization, you've got to foster cooperation toward achieving common goals or business results…whatever it is the organization defines as 'success.'"

"That's right. And those common goals could cover anything from producing quality pet supplies to developing software to mobilizing volunteers for some philanthropic cause. Communication is the cornerstone of cooperation. You simply cannot have cooperation without it. And if you can't have cooperation, you might as well work alone."

Jerry continued.

"There are five key elements to effective communication. They're easy to remember because they all begin with the letter 'P.' The first 'P' stands for *principles*…the foundational values that determine the way we deal with others. The principles that drive our communication model are respect, honesty, clarity, and responsibility."

"What's so special about those four principles?" asked another student. "Why not efficiency, or speed, or diversity?"

"Those are all good things, too. But they're not as critical to communication as the other four. If you hold others in high esteem, deal with them honestly, try to be as clear as possible, and assign responsibility where it most sensibly belongs, then you have the foundation for strong organizational communication. Not just internally, but with external customers as well. Wanda just told us the role of communication is to foster cooperation toward achieving goals and results. You see, treating others with respect and honesty will get you on your way toward the first half of the equation—because they foster trust and cooperation. Similarly, clarity and responsibility are the chief drivers of the second half of the equation—the goals and results. So in approaching any business communication, you want to start with these four principles."

The next 'P' stands for *purpose*. Once you've gotten the principles down, you should ask yourself, 'What am I trying to accomplish here?' This step is helpful for maintaining a results focus. I once worked on a loading dock and used to constantly whine to my co-workers about the inefficiency of the process. It wasn't until a good friend challenged my whining that I realized if I wanted to see the process improve, I had to talk to management in a constructive way. She helped me see that merely complaining to my co-workers was a waste of time and breath. And since I'm a dog, nobody wants more of *my* breath than they absolutely have to endure.

"Asking the purpose question helps assure proper intention, which increases the likelihood that you'll achieve your desired result. It will keep you focused on your priorities and remind you to put effort into both transmitting and receiving. When you ask the purpose question, you may end up concluding that the best option is to keep your mouth and ears closed. The most obvious example of this is gossiping about a co-worker. Gossiping rarely grows from a constructive purpose and almost never produces a desirable outcome.

Jerry continued, "The third 'P' stands for *players*. After dealing with principles and purpose, you next want to ask yourself: 'Which players need to be involved, and to what extent, in order to accomplish my purpose?' and 'Who is in the best position to deliver the message?'"

Jerry fielded some questions at that point as the students began to discover how they might apply what they were learning to schoolwork, social lives, and potential business situations. Even the students who had initially been insensitive and rude to Jerry were beginning to show some interest. Perhaps Jerry was winning their respect.

"The fourth, and perhaps most complex element of the model is *presentation*. The question here is *How* should I deliver the message?' This is where you not only identify the core message—the key idea you are trying to convey or accurately receive—but also where you decide how to package the exchange for maximal effectiveness. So, as you can see from the diagram, the packaging that surrounds the core message includes all the subtleties necessary to accomplish an effective delivery."

Jerry spent a good portion of his talk fleshing out this particular aspect of communication effectiveness. He used his experiences at SCRAPPI and the lessons he learned from Sophia to help the students understand. He taught them the importance of choosing the best mode, attending to non-verbals, and placing a message in its proper context. The students learned the value of timing, empathic listening, choosing the right turf, and regulating the emotional intensity of an exchange. Most importantly, Jerry taught them about behavioral integrity—ensuring consistency between one's words and one's actions.

"So often," he said, "Communicators do well with the core message, but package things so poorly that cooperation and results go right out the window."

Jerry went on. "The fifth and final element is *proof.* Here, you ask the question: 'Did the message get through?' Look for ways to verify the message was received as it was intended. If so, great. Then you can move onto something else. If not, then you've still got work to do—but at least you won't get stuck operating under false information or assumptions."

The Junior Business Achievers seemed to grasp Jerry's model and to enjoy learning about workplace communication. They asked a number of questions and worked through several scenarios together to get a practical sense of applying the model in their own lives.

After Jerry's concluding remarks, several students remained to take advantage of his availability. Indeed, things had turned out much better than Jerry thought. By this point, he was actually glad to be sentenced to community service. It proved valuable to the students…and to Jerry himself.

It was getting late, and Jerry's stomach was communicating its need for food. Jerry also wanted some time with Sophia to hear what she thought of his presentation. So he invited her to the restaurant at the hotel for coffee and dessert. For the first time since Jerry had known her, Sophia made herself visible to everyone else. Jerry wasn't sure why, but he figured something had forever changed in their relationship. And wouldn't you know it— Deliscuit cookies were featured on the dessert tray that evening. It was fitting, Jerry thought. The cookies reminded him of how he first met Sophia, and of how far they had come together.

Sophia expressed her approval of Jerry's presentation. She offered genuine praise, along with a few points of constructive feedback. There was silence for a moment, which Sophia broke with the words, "I'm not sure you need me much any more, Jerry."

Jerry looked at the floor. He had trouble knowing what to say.

After an uncomfortable silence, Sophia said, "Speak, Mulligan! What's on your mind?"

"Sophia," Jerry began, "I wouldn't be where I am today if it hadn't been for your guidance." He paused and sniffled, and dabbed the corner of his eye with his paw. "How can I ever thank you?"

"Just seeing you grow into a capable leader and effective communicator has been enough reward for me," Sophia said, struggling herself to restrain the tears that were beginning to well in her eyes.

When writing a humorous book about communication, don't ruin it by getting sappy at the end.

"Sophia," Jerry began, "I wouldn't be where I am today if it hadn't been for your guidance." He paused and sniffled, and dabbed the corner of his eye with his paw. "How can I ever thank you?"

"Well, first you can pay the bill!" Sophia said, as she slid the check toward the downcast dog.

At that very moment, their attentive, yet intrusive waiter, interrupted to admonish the sullen setter, "Pull yourself together, Buddy! I haven't seen a mutt blubber like you since that *Lassie* episode when Timmy got lost in the woods!"

Jerry cracked a smile, recalculated the tip, and thanked the waiter for his "kind advice."

"You *are* a piece of work, Jerry Mulligan," Sophia chuckled. "But I have to admit this has been rewarding for me as well. You've come a long way. Now you need to take some concrete measures to ensure you further develop and maintain the skills you've learned. Review the key communication truths we have discovered. Talk with your co-workers...peers, supervisors, and subordinates...and seek their input on how effectively you employ these communication ideals. Once you've gathered feedback, set specific goals for improvement, and find someone who is willing to hold you accountable for accomplishing them. Re-measure your performance periodically. If you're serious about professional development, and if you grasp the importance of effective communication, then you'll do more than just shelve my words. You will discipline yourself to continuously sharpen your communication skills."

> # For your new communication skills to take hold, you must put them into practice and constantly refine them.

Mulligan's Mull-Agains

1. What steps should I take to ensure that my completion of this book will not be the final chapter in my development as an effective communicator?

Author's Note

The Association for Humane Treatment of Animals monitored the animal action in this book. No animal was harmed. Narratives appearing to place animals in jeopardy were simulated.

Appendix: Mulligan's Model for Communication Effectiveness

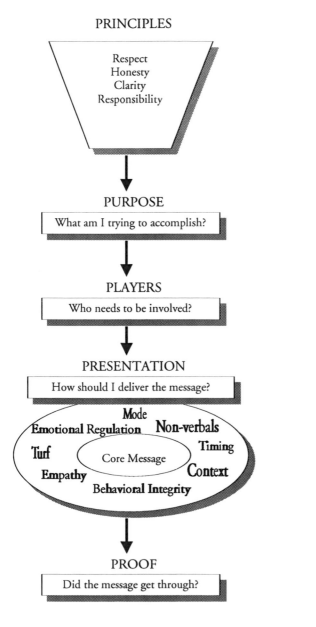

PRINCIPLES

Respect
Honesty
Clarity
Responsibility

Drives healthy organizational communication by fostering cooperation, trust, and results-focus.

PURPOSE

What am I trying to accomplish?

Encourages intention, prioritization, and results-focus.

PLAYERS

Who needs to be involved?

Directs the message to where it can be most useful.

PRESENTATION

How should I deliver the message?

Packages the exchange for maximal effectiveness and minimal undesirable side effects.

Mode
Emotional Regulation Non-verbals
Turf Timing
Core Message
Empathy Context
Behavioral Integrity

PROOF

Did the message get through?

Verifies the message was received as intended.

0-595-30658-6

CPSIA information can be obtained at www.ICGtesting.com
Printed in the USA
BVOW03s0136260713

326887BV00002B/109/A